An Apuleius Reader

Bc LATIN Readers

Series Editor:
Ronnie Ancona, Hunter College and CUNY Graduate Center

These readers provide well annotated Latin selections written by experts in the field, to be used as authoritative introductions to Latin authors, genres, topics, or themes for intermediate or advanced college Latin study. Their relatively small size (covering 500–600 lines) makes them ideal to use in combination. Each volume includes a comprehensive introduction, bibliography for further reading, Latin text with notes at the back, and complete vocabulary. Nineteen volumes are currently scheduled for publication; others are under consideration. Check our website for updates: www.BOLCHAZY.com.

An Apuleius Reader

Selections from the *Metamorphoses*

Ellen D. Finkelpearl

Bolchazy-Carducci Publishers, Inc.
Wauconda, Illinois USA

Series Editor: Ronnie Ancona
Volume Editor: Laurie Haight Keenan
Cover Design & Typography: Adam Phillip Velez
Maps: Mapping Specialists, Ltd.

An Apuleius Reader
Selections from the Metamorphoses

Ellen D. Finkelpearl

Bolchazy-Carducci Publishers, Inc.
1000 Brown Street
Wauconda, Illinois 60084
www.bolchazy.com

Printed in the United States of America
2022
by Publishers' Graphics

ISBN 978-0-86516-714-8

Library of Congress Cataloging-in-Publication Data

Apuleius.
  [Metamorphoses. Selections]
 An Apuleius reader : selections from the Metamorphoses / Ellen D. Finkelpearl.
    pages. cm. -- (BC Latin readers)
  ISBN 978-0-86516-714-8 (pbk. : alk. paper) 1. Apuleius. Metamorphoses. I. Finkelpearl,
Ellen D., 1953- II. Title. III. Series: BC Latin readers.
  PA6207.M33F56 2012
  873'.01--dc23

                                                                        2012023274

Contents

List of Illustrations

Preface

Apuleius is certainly one of the most entertaining of ancient authors and has undergone a renaissance in popularity in the last several decades, but has not been read much at an undergraduate level because of his difficulty and the dearth of affordable and concise commentaries. This is unfortunate because he offers something for every reader: transformations and magic, travel and adventure, robbers and slaves, not to mention philosophy and religion. I hope that this *libellus* will give more students the chance to read this amazing author.

It is difficult to excerpt an author one thinks of as saying everything there is to say in the world. The Bolchazy-Carducci Latin Readers are short! The selections I have made represent a compromise, one between simply including all of my favorite passages and presenting a text that preserves the narrative of the story of Lucius (and that of Psyche), as well as some of the more famous and striking passages. For this reason as well, the selections in the Reader are limited to the *Metamorphoses*, despite increasing scholarly attention to and appreciation of the rhetorical and philosophical works. Although my instinct was to avoid portions that already are treated in commentaries appropriate for use in the classroom, in the end it seemed to be in the spirit of the series simply to choose the most important and interesting passages. I have, however, avoided most of Book 1 in the hope that this Reader will be used in classrooms in conjunction with Ruebel's Bolchazy-Carducci commentary on Book 1. This combination would also provide more exposure to the embedded tales.

The book is designed for upper intermediate to advanced students. I have not changed any of the Latin, unlike the recent collection of excerpts by Murgatroyd (Cambridge 2009) or the Balme and Morwood adapted *Cupid and Psyche* (Oxford). While Apuleius' Latin is odd, it is certainly more Latin than anything we create now.

I would particularly like to thank my excellent students Caroline Mahoney and Julia Mebane of Scripps College—Caroline painstakingly inserted all the macrons in the lexicon and Julie offered especially detailed feedback on an early version of the commentary. Ilsa Lund provided crucial formatting assistance and moral support; I am grateful to the Latin class of David Clark at Hunter College, which also tried out the commentary and caught some errors, and to the anonymous readers of the manuscript, one of whom sent back extremely detailed comments. Ronnie Ancona and Laurie Haight Keenan have been the most supportive and responsive of editors and I owe them many debts of thanks.

Most of all, I thank my parents for instilling in my brother and me a love of learning and the arts and, in my case, the Classics. My father taught me my first Latin and my mother even studied Xenophon in Greek—and they have given unfailing support in other ways. This book is dedicated to them.

Introduction

∾ Apuleius' life and works

It is common to introduce Apuleius to the newcomer with his own words: *lector intende, laetaberis* ("pay attention, reader, you will be delighted"). The critical trope is old but no less true for being worn. The reader may not be delighted in any ordinary sense; the speaker sometimes announces a "charming tale" only to kill off most of its characters by the end, and provides laughter with a heavy dose of cruelty; the entertainment consists more often of dark surrealism than light silliness. Yet, whether he describes the erotics of cooking, the depressing plight of slaves in the mill, or Lucius' new-found spirituality, Apuleius is among the most fascinating of ancient authors.

Fig. 1 Portrait generally considered to be Apuleius, fourth century CE. Trier Museum, Germany. Wikimedia Commons.

Apuleius (possibly Lucius Apuleius) was born in the mid-120s CE (under Hadrian) in Madauros in Africa Proconsularis (now M'Dauorouch in Algeria) of an elite family with substantial wealth. He studied first in Carthage (about 150 miles to the northeast) and later in Athens for further education in philosophy and rhetoric. The culture in which he grew up was therefore mixed; Punic was the vernacular language of the area, the language in use before colonization by the Romans, and many locals did not speak Latin. Apuleius never directly mentions speaking Punic himself, but it was doubtless his first language, along with Latin. He later acquired Greek, as was common for the educated, and was thus trilingual. The cultural background to Apuleius' works, then, included immersion in all aspects of Graeco-Roman culture, but was not identical to that of Vergil or Ovid. As Bradley, in particular, has emphasized, Apuleius was surrounded by markers of indigenous culture: bilingual Punic and Latin inscriptions, temples to Punic gods like Tanit, mosaics and architecture not Roman alone in style. Libyan culture was also strong in the area. What was Apuleius' ethnicity—descendent of Roman settlers or of local ancestry? He identifies himself in the *Apology* as "semi-Numidian, semi-Gaetulian" (*Apol.* 24), which may well refer to his ancestry rather than just the location of his hometown (see further Finkelpearl 2009).

According to the *Apology*, Apuleius married a woman significantly older than himself, Aemilia Pudentilla, thus inheriting her wealth and precipitating a law suit by her in-laws who accused him of having won her affections by magic. Apuleius' *Apology* is the speech allegedly delivered on this occasion in another North African town, Sabratha, several hundred miles to the south. Apuleius' *Apology* is an amusing defense that incorporates poems of Catullus, lore about crocodiles, and interesting tidbits about ancient magical practices. It is the one work of Apuleius that can be dated with any certainty; it was delivered before Claudius Maximus, who was proconsul of Africa in 158/9 CE.

Although the *Metamorphoses* is the work of Apuleius best known today, he was famous in his day more as a rhetorician and philosopher. The *Florida*, a collection of excerpts from his "epideictic" oratory (i.e., speeches for entertainment rather than serious forensic speeches), survives and gives a sense of the range of catchy, learned, often philosophically based speeches that Apuleius delivered as a "sophist" travelling the Mediterranean, entertaining crowds. The diverse topics of these twenty-three excerpts include the musical contest between Marsyas and Apollo (*Florida* 3), the speech patterns of the parrot (12), Crates' rejection of material wealth (14), and the travels of Pythagoras to visit Zoroaster and other eastern sages (14). At various points in the *Metamorphoses*, one can see this rhetorical training and practice surfacing—for example, in the trial scene of the Risus Festival of Book 3 or the description of Cupid's hair in Book 5.

Apuleius was important enough as a philosopher to have earned at least one statue in his honor, proclaiming him to be a "Platonic Philosopher." He was part of the philosophical movement known as "Middle Platonism," which continued to develop the ideas of Plato from the first century BCE to the third century CE. One of the central tenets, which Apuleius explains in the *De Deo Socratis*, is that God or the gods are transcendent and unapproachable but that beings called "*daimones*" function as intermediaries between humans and the gods. (See Dillon 1996.) In the *De Deo Socratis* Apuleius discourses on Socrates' *daimonion*, the guardian spirit that advised Socrates. He also translated Plato's *Phaedo* into Latin, but that work is lost. A work plausibly attributed to Apuleius, the *De Platone*, explains Platonic philosophy in two books. Other philosophy includes the *De Mundo*, a Latin version of the pseudo-Aristotelian *Peri Kosmou*, and the *Peri Hermeneias*, a work on formal logic. Of questioned authenticity is the *Asclepius*, a Hermetic treatise.

As is so common in Classics, a large number of Apuleius' other varied works has been lost: another novel called the *Hermagoras*, works on proverbs, a whole discourse on fish (*De Piscibus*), treatises on agriculture, astronomy, music (a topic that appears frequently in his works), botany, poetry, arithmetic, a work called the *Eroticus*, and an epitome of history.

He was, in other words, a polymath, an intellectual of great versatility, though many scholars paint him as more of a showman than a genuine philosopher or intellectual, excessively proud of the breadth of his knowledge, but shallow. This may be unfair. These days, it is common to think of him as part of an intellectual movement existing primarily in the Greek world, referred to as the "Second Sophistic" (following Philostratus, a philosopher/biographer of the late second century CE), a revival in the second and third centuries CE of the intellectual flourishing of fifth-century Athens. Much of the work associated with this movement is rhetorical and performative, often flamboyant, often concerned with negotiating the relationship between the political dominance of Rome and the intellectual superiority of Greece and with defining new ways of being Greek in changed political and cultural circumstances (Whitmarsh 1999). Insofar as Apuleius was part of this coterie, educated as he was in Athens under and with many practicing Greek sophists (on which, see Sandy 1997), he is still a Latin sophist (see Harrison 2000) and a North African, reshaping the new intellectual traditions in ways that still need to be defined further.

In short, Apuleius worked in an eclectic environment in many different senses and produced an astounding array of intellectual works. He stood at a crossroads of culture, not only geographically, but chronologically, at the moment when the old religions were giving way to the introduction of Christianity. Many of the areas of interest and expertise touched on above will crop up throughout the *Metamorphoses*, which some have argued is the final, mature work of his career, though the date is unclear—probably after the *Apology* since it is not mentioned in that defense, and maybe as late as the 170s or 180s CE. There is no evidence to supply the date of his death.

❧ *The* METAMORPHOSES *or* GOLDEN ASS

The title of this work is unclear; *Metamorphoses* appears in the manuscripts, while *Asinus Aureus* is attested in a reference to the work by St. Augustine with the phrase, "in the books which he inscribed with the title 'Asinus Aureus'" (*City of God* 18,18). Thus, both titles seem to be original. The precise significance of "golden" in the title is obscure and seems paradoxical since asses were cheap and lowly animals, but probably refers to the wondrousness of the story. Most Classicists refer to the text as the *Metamorphoses*, while most non-Classicists call it the *Golden Ass*. (See further Bitel 2000–2001.)

The basic story is simple: an aristocratic Greek youth named Lucius travels to Thessaly in search of adventure and magic. He stays with a man whose wife is a witch and becomes involved with their slave, Fotis, through whom he is introduced to magic and is accidentally transformed into a donkey. (Note that "donkey" and "ass" are the same animal; a "mule" is a sterile hybrid produced by the mating of a donkey and a horse, used commonly for heavy work in antiquity.). Although the antidote—roses—is apparently easy to come by, he spends the next seven books (most of the work) as a donkey. As that servile animal, he carries loads, is beaten and abused, sinks into poverty and despair, and later becomes a source of entertainment, slated to be a spectacle in the amphitheater. Finally, in Book 11, he comes upon a festival for the Egyptian goddess, Isis. Under her protection, he eats roses and is re-transformed. He then becomes her devotee and priest, and later is initiated into associated Egyptian cults. However, the frame narrative is complicated by the interlacing of numerous "embedded" or "inserted" tales including the well-known "Tale of Cupid and Psyche," many of which are only loosely connected to Lucius' adventures. The work has also seemed enigmatic and scattered because of its unexpected religious conclusion. We will return to these questions shortly.

∾ *Background*

Generically, the *Metamorphoses* is usually grouped with the other works considered the classic examples of the "ancient novel," a literary form that, by ancient standards, did not have a long history like epic, for example. The Greek side is represented by five novels of love and adventure: *Chaereas and Callirhoe* by Chariton, *An Ephesian Tale* by Xenophon of Ephesus, *Daphnis and Chloe* by Longus, *Leucippe and Clitophon* by Achilles Tatius, and *An Ethiopian Story* by Heliodorus (conveniently collected in Reardon 1989). Their dating is unusually problematic. Current thinking inclines to place the earliest of the extant Greek works (Chariton) in the mid-first century CE and the latest (Heliodorus) in the fourth century, but arguments have been made for a beginning of the genre in the first century BCE (see Bowie 2002). In any case, the form seems to have flourished in the heyday of the Roman Empire and the late days of paganism. Despite fundamental differences in length, sophistication, and quality, the Greek novels have remarkably similar plots: a supernaturally beautiful boy and girl meet, fall in love, are separated and go through arduous trials, but are reunited, return "home" in various senses, and are reintegrated into society. Abduction by pirates, shipwreck, travel to the exotic east, and attempted seduction by rivals are common features (less so in *Daphnis and Chloe*). In Latin, the *Metamorphoses* and Petronius' *Satyricon* (first century CE) are the main representatives of the genre, though the anonymous *History of Apollonius King of Tyre*, late, brief, and possibly of Greek origin, may be grouped with them. Yet, "novel" is problematic from several points of view; not only do modern scholars (particularly outside Classics), question the designation of these works as "novels," in comparison with the more developed form of the modern novel, but there was no actual term for the genre (if it is one) in antiquity, and its origins are unknown. Nor is it clear whether an ancient reader (or maybe a modern reader, either) would have thought of, e.g., *Daphnis and Chloe* and the *Satyricon* as generically linked. It is also unclear whether there is any direct filiation between the ancient and modern novel (on which see Doody 1996).

It is becoming more popular now to include these works within a broader category, "prose fiction," or even "ancient narrative"—what is a novel, after all?—that encompasses as well such works as Christian saints' lives, Lucian's dialogues, Plutarch's more fanciful treatises, and ancient biography. This shift to include "the fringe" also recognizes the origins of the "novel" in the fictional histories of Herodotus, for example, or the storytelling elements of Plato's dialogues. For while poetry had been more specifically the province of fiction, prose had also more subtly been home to storytelling.

The most immediate source for Apuleius' *Metamorphoses* is, apparently, a Greek original *Metamorphoseis*, now lost. There exists, however, preserved among the works of Lucian (second century CE) an ass-tale (included in Reardon 1989 by the name "The Ass") that scholars generally agree is a shortened version of the above. (For a brief discussion, see Harrison 1996, 500–502.) The precise nature of the longer original that may have been Apuleius' source is impossible to recover, but the extant *Onos* (the Greek name for "The Ass") is strikingly similar to Apuleius' *Metamorphoses* in outline: a young man named Lukios sets out for Thessaly on business and is transformed into an ass. The narrative of the *Onos* is similarly first-person and the adventures that Lukios himself encounters are sometimes almost identical to those of Lucius in Apuleius, even to the point of wording (though the *Onos* is, of course, in Greek). The important difference is that the Greek story as it survives includes none of the embedded tales found in Apuleius (no *Cupid and Psyche*, for example) and lacks the religious ending. Instead, after Lukios is restored to human form, the woman who had been erotically involved with him as ass rejects him for his reduced sexual potency. It is impossible to tell whether the longer Greek original involved embedded tales or not.

Most scholars note the crude style and unsophisticated narrative of the *Onos* compared to Apuleius' *Metamorphoses*, and it is important to keep in mind that Apuleius clearly innovated and embellished the Greek story and radically changed its tone by adding the Isiac conclusion. However, the *Onos* exhibits an interestingly oppositional stance toward the Roman occupation of Greece, providing a first-person, often subversive narrative about Roman power and social institutions more generally. In one scene, a Roman soldier tries to steal Lukios the ass from his Greek master, imperialistically speaking Latin to the uncomprehending Greek gardener who owns Lukios, but the gardener manages to get the better of the soldier and beats him almost to death (*Onos* 44). Clearly, the scene both exposes the arrogance of Roman occupying soldiers and offers a satisfying example of revenge, enjoyable to the Greek audience. This scene is imitated and embellished in Apuleius (9.39), preserving the oppositional stance toward Rome. (See Hall 1995, Finkelpearl 2007.) As Edith Hall argues, the basic structure of the story, in which an aristocratic youth is housed in the body of the lowest creature, provides a "double vision" of social norms, that of the elite and of the slave. Thus, the story already questions social assumptions and hierarchies even before Apuleius modifies it.

∾ Interpreting the METAMORPHOSES

One common way of reading the *Metamorphoses* is to see it as a moral tale of fall and redemption: Lucius indulges in forbidden *curiositas* about magic while also engaging in an erotic liaison with a slave; embedded tales in Books 1 and 2 should have alerted him to the dangers of his desire(s), but he is headstrong and reaps the rewards; he is punished by transformation into an animal known for its lust, and, after sufficient suffering, is saved by the divine intervention of Isis, perhaps more a result of simple grace than by virtue of having learned or improved morally. This is essentially the reading proposed by the priest in Book 11 (see selection with notes). Sometimes this reading is given a Platonic slant in recognition of Apuleius' known Platonism. In his *Symposium* and *Phaedrus*, Plato (via Socrates) describes a process whereby the soul gazing on beauty and feeling desire/love (*eros*) for beauty ascends a ladder until it reaches a divine state of transcendence in the company of Beauty pure and unattached to the physical world. In the *Metamorphoses*, Isis comes to represent the form of Beauty and Truth, the light after the darkness of Lucius' ignorance and interest in the wrong kind of knowledge, or a *daimon*, an intermediary through whom Lucius has contact with the divine. She is associated with *providentia*, a power more beneficent than Fate in Platonic/Middle Platonic thinking. The "Tale of Cupid and Psyche" in this reading is a prototype of Lucius' experiences; Psyche, too, falls through unholy *curiositas* in her desire to look upon the forbidden divine and is similarly redeemed. The naming of the characters Cupid and Psyche, love and the soul, gives an even more clearly Platonic meaning to the tale.

The reading just outlined gives a satisfying moral coherence to the *Metamorphoses* and has a certain truth to it, yet (to my mind) misses the essential texture and outlook of the book, which involves a fundamental destabilizing of the world. Lucius (as well as Aristomenes and Socrates of Book 1) has set out on business (1.2: *Thessaliam ex negotio petebam*), but (albeit willingly) encounters transformative magic, which pulls apart the certainties of life as we know it. In his search for magic, Lucius has a vision of the world (2.1) in which he believes that nothing is as it seems; reality and illusion are indistinguishable; trees are probably transformed humans. In this confused, surreal world, and through circumstances just as surreal, Lucius becomes a laughingstock of the entire city of Hypata. The world of this apparently privileged youth has become cruel, its citizens sadistic, as they watch Lucius suffer, and laugh.

The culmination of these instabilities is, of course, Lucius' transformation into an ass (3.24–25), but along with this transformation comes an unsettling of one of the distinctions most fundamental to human existence: our difference from animals. Lucius is neither human nor animal, but also both. He thinks like a human, but sometimes that human thinking looks very much like ass-thought. At 4.4–5, we see this ambiguity, which appears in a different way in Book 10 (10.16–17) when Lucius is partially reintegrated into human society, performing human tricks and acting as a remarkably intelligent ass. These confusions are not only comic (and that is not to be underestimated), but also demolish the set categories that structure our world, providing shifting points of reference. The story is being told, it should be remembered, from the point of view of the experiencing ass, though obviously (within the fiction) written by Lucius after recovering his human form. Thus, the narrative retains the "double consciousness" described above in relation to the *Onos*.

Double consciousness is not all, for something like half the book is narrated by others. In this book of excerpts, the only embedded tale represented is the "Tale of Cupid and Psyche," but the *Metamorphoses* is narrated by a variety of voices to a variety of audiences: travelling salesmen victimized by witches, the drunken old woman who tells the tale of Psyche, robbers in their den, a slave-overseer, an old "madam" fixing up adulterous liaisons, and more. Sometimes we are given narratives within narratives within the narrative by

Lucius, so that the book is polyvocal, not presented from a single perspective, deliberately reminding the audience that there is never any one single point of view.

Narration "from below," by slaves, robbers, and the victimized, is one of the more remarkable features of the *Metamorphoses*. In particular, the book describes from the inside what it is like to be forced to do menial tasks like carrying wood from the mountain, how it feels to be beaten at the whim of one's master or to be subjected to life in the mill, walking around in circles grinding grain. As a donkey, Lucius is entirely in the power and at the mercy of his owners, some of whom are kindly, but most of whom treat him wretchedly. As Bradley, Fitzgerald, and others have pointed out, Lucius' life as an animal closely resembles the plight of a slave. Normally, though, we do not hear about the lives of slaves, so numerous in the ancient world, from their point of view. Slaves tend to be treated as silent and invisible presences to be ignored by the free. The passage in Book 9 (9.12–13) is an exceptional glimpse into the grim realities of slavery, and offers a direct connection between the condition of slavery and that of the animal. There is, then, an unmasking or questioning of the established social hierarchies and the organization of society, connected to (though different from) the kinds of instability outlined above, though Apuleius' motives in this regard are unclear, as he was himself the owner of numerous slaves.

Normative and singular points of reference are further dislodged in the treatment of gender in the *Metamorphoses*. In Book 11, it is not Jupiter or Apollo who saves Lucius, but Isis, a female deity who claims (at 11.5) to manifest in her one person all the forms of gods and goddesses. She is later supplanted (in ways problematic for interpretation) by Osiris, but it is Isis who forms the focus of the bulk of Book 11, Isis who effects a profound spiritual experience in Lucius. The "Tale of Cupid and Psyche" is completely female-centered; the teller, addressee, the protagonist and the antagonist (Venus) are all female. The protagonist has only sisters. A daughter is born. The labors imposed on Psyche are all female ones, involving cooking (separating the grains), cloth-making (gathering the fleece), drawing water, and cosmetics (bringing back Proserpina's beauty). The story is something of a female fantasy—Psyche is so beautiful that even Cupid cannot resist—and, like a Jane Austen novel, ends in marriage. (Still, to some people's taste, the heroine is a bit passive.) An audience accustomed to a male point of view listens to a female voice for a full quarter of the book. Some of the females in the *Metamorphoses* are evil and lustful—the witches and the adulterous women of the later books in particular—but they always have agency. For some reason as well, Lucius traces his family relationship to Plutarch through his mother (1.2) and the book is filled with small details that take account of the female.

Additionally, the world of the *Metamorphoses* is shaken up by a cultural re-orientation. The work does begin and end with Rome, yet Latin is called *"exoticus"* (1.1) and the speaker refers to himself as someone whose Latin is faulty. Gone is the kind of assumption that one finds in Vergil, that Rome is, without question, the center of the world and was divinely intended to be so. Lucius wanders all over the Greek world and ends up in Rome, but his Rome is not the Rome of the Senate House and the Capitoline Hill, but rather has its center in the Temple of Isis where Lucius goes daily to worship a foreign goddess. He does become an advocate in the courts of Rome (11.30), but is, for reasons unexplained, the subject of envy, giving us the sense, as the work closes, that he is a misfit among Romans rather than a happily assimilated Romano-Greek, as he wanders around Rome joyfully with an Isiac shaven head. How much does this de-centering of Rome have to do with the foreign origins of its author? Apuleius enigmatically introduces his own birthplace, Madauros in North Africa, into the text at 11.27 where a priest of Isis dreams that a man from Madauros will be sent to him—meaning Lucius, no doubt, but deliberately confusing the two. In any case, the introduction of Madauros as Lucius' birthplace provides another non-Roman marker. (On the complex question of Apuleius and his North African identity, see further Finkelpearl 2009.)

Yet another anomalous feature of this text is its spirituality. Lucius' emotional ties to Isis may seem familiar to us from the example of Christianity, but the kind of life-changing, all-encompassing devotion that Lucius demonstrates (some chapters not excerpted here)

is not the norm for pagan worship. It is in this new kind of spiritual-
ity and "conversion" that Lucius finds stability and control over the
irrational forces that have been throwing his world into confusion
(Shumate 1996).

In short, this is a strange and rather subversive book that focuses
on a departure from normative ways of structuring the world, in-
clusion of a multitude of voices, bizarre and comical juxtapositions
and disjunctions, a dark view of humanity, dethroning of figures in
power, decentering, and finally new ways toward joy. Such an ob-
servation does not preclude a moral interpretation of the sort with
which this section began: in a cruel and disordered world, Lucius
falls through curiosity, is punished, and so on. Yet, apart from the
fact that there seems to be a disjunction here between the opaque
complexity, surreal comedy, and persistent questioning that Apu-
leius presents and the neat, closed solution that the moral reading
offers (and with a hint of suspicious influence from our ingrained
Judeo-Christian worldview), it is important to note where Lucius
ends up. The ending (and we will return to conflicting interpreta-
tions in a moment) emphatically does not put Lucius back where he
started. If what we were reading was simply a morality tale about
Lucius and his faults, one would expect him to be reintegrated into
his previous life, wiser and ready to live according to established
social and moral rules. Instead, Lucius finds himself in a complete-
ly different world, under the protection of a goddess he apparently
knew nothing about, a *goddess*, who structures his life differently,
including many moments of silent contemplation and devotion in
a closed community. The introduction of a foreign religion leads
to a reshaping of categories; gods may be part animal (e.g., Anubis
with his dog's head); society is organized not according to politi-
cal nations, but according to communities of Isis; slavery has been
modified, at least in Lucius' case, to mean a voluntary slavery to
the goddess; magic is subsumed under the divine. Perhaps what the
text most addresses is the possibility of dismantling the world and
reshaping it in other ways—an appropriate focus for a work called
Metamorphoses.

ᔆ *Other readings*

One extremely influential reading of the *Metamorphoses* is J. J. Win-
kler's *Auctor & Actor: A Narratological Reading of Apuleius's Golden
Ass* (1985). Winkler examines the gap between Lucius as "actor" or
the "I" experiencing the events and as "auctor," the ultimate author
or relator of events. One expects some kind of retrospection by the
auctor at the end of the work, Winkler argues, that would analyze
the experiences of the *actor* in terms of the changed identity of the
speaker. In the parallel case of St. Augustine's *Confessions*, the narra-
tion of pre-conversion life is constantly interwoven with comments
by the *auctor* judging the emptiness of that life without God. One
might expect Lucius the Isiac priest recording the events for us to
cast that kind of critical eye on his life before Isis, but he never does.
The narrative therefore is never brought full circle, the experienc-
es never scrutinized by the first-person narrator; instead the story
consists largely of a series of events told naively as they were experi-
enced. The text is therefore open and "unauthorized." As part of this
reading, Winkler also drew attention to some unsettling features of
the ending. After Lucius has been initiated into the cult of Isis, in the
last four sections of the work (11.26.4–11.30), he begins to have more
dreams and visions and is initiated twice more into associated Egyp-
tian cults. Lucius is forced even to sell his clothes in order to afford
the final initiation. Questions arise over whether he is being duped
by money-grubbing priests and is prey to the attractions of any new
cult. Winkler suggested that both a reading satiric of Lucius and his
conversion and a serious reading of that experience are available and
that different readers will seize on one or the other.

In a reading focused on conversion, Nancy Shumate (1996) looks
at the bewildering worldview that Winkler had described and argues
that Lucius is undergoing "epistemic rupture." The ways he under-
stands the world are failing him; he needs new frames of reference
and anchors; he has pursued false values and ultimately finds salva-
tion through true values with Isis. Shumate compares Lucius' pre-
conversion experience with modern conversion narratives to show
that this collapse in frames of reference undergone by Lucius closely

parallels that of the modern pre-convert. In response to the moraliz-
ing reading of the work, she argues that Lucius' crisis is not primarily
moral, but epistemic or cognitive. He needs a new set of values and a
new way to structure his world. In Isis he finds stability and coher-
ence. General discussion above is heavily influenced by Shumate's
analysis of the dissolution of Lucius' world.

More recently, many critics have adopted only the satiric part
of Winkler's analysis—Lucius is a credulous fool, under the influ-
ence of trickster priests and has learned nothing from his experi-
ences (e.g., van Mal-Maeder 1997; Harrison 2000). The entire novel
is "comic" rather than a comic work with a serious ending and a
redemptive experience; there is no disjunction in tone between the
first ten books and the final one. Kenney (2003) suggests that Lucius-
auctor, now older and wiser, may be looking back on his adventures
and exposing his previous foolishness as a cult follower. He supports
this reading by interpreting the passage at 9.13 in which Lucius looks
back at his travels and opines that they rendered him "*multiscium
sed minus prudentem*" ("full of knowledge but not very wise," as he
translates it, but see notes to the passage). The statement that Lucius
has been rendered "not very wise" is taken as an interpretation of the
entire experience of Lucius, including his later conversion. It must
be admitted that the last few chapters do present a problem for those
who read the conversion to the Isis cult as an expression by Apuleius
of a straightforwardly devout and uncomplicated religious experi-
ence. However, the dream vision of Isis and the devotion by Lucius
in the first twelve chapters of Book 11 are so moving and heartfelt
and so astounding as a religious experience in the pagan world, that
it seems equally tunnel-visioned to ignore that part of the picture. A
number of essays in the recent volume, *Aspects of Apuleius' Golden
Ass III: The Isis-Book*, emphasize the various ways that Book 11 is not
serious alone, but also light and playful and satiric. Criticism seems
to be moving toward an awareness of the coexistence of the comic
and serious in the novel's conclusion.

Finally, this book has often been read as some kind of strange
autobiography. (St. Augustine believed that it was Apuleius who
had turned into an ass, an extreme version of the autobiographical

reading!) Lucius' designation as "the man from Madauros," which was Apuleius' birthplace (11.27), the first person narration, and the fact that the manuscripts give Apuleius' praenomen as "Lucius" all lead the reader to feel that this is a story of a personal journey of some kind (not literal, of course). Psychologists have approached the text, especially the "Tale of Cupid and Psyche," in great numbers, as it lends itself to symbolic readings and has the quality of a dream (on which see Gollnick 1992). In this case, we may read Lucius as a satiric version of Apuleius himself, yet the satire loses some of its bite. As Harrison (2000) emphasizes, there is much about Lucius' self-presentation as someone of education and *doctrina* that resonates with the life of Apuleius himself. Perhaps the particular nature of an autobiographical reading is best left to the imagination of readers.

ᴄᴠ *Cupid and Psyche*

In the middle of Lucius' travels as an ass, he is taken to a robbers' den. Soon, a girl named Charite, abducted from her very wedding, is brought to the cave where she begins to lament her fate. A drunken old woman who tends to the robbers tries to console her by telling her the "Tale of Cupid and Psyche." The context is important because we should keep in mind the embedded audience of the tale, a young girl not unlike Psyche. The tale is well known today and often excerpted or retold without any reference to Apuleius as source, sometimes referred to as a "Greek myth." In fact, Apuleius' *Metamorphoses* is the only ancient source for the narrative, nor are there any fragments or ancient references to any other written version, as is often the case with ancient texts. There are, however, numerous visual representations of the two, dating from the third century BCE, Cupid with bird wings and Psyche with butterfly wings (Psyche means both "soul" and "butterfly" in Greek). By Apuleius' time, Cupid and Psyche are popular on funerary reliefs and sarcophagi, apparently with religious significance as emblems of salvation, and it is likely that some kind of oral tradition surrounded these figures. Yet the pairing of the two figures does not constitute the kind of narrative found in Apuleius, including, for example, all the labors of Psyche or the anger of Venus,

according to Schlam (1976). The most we can say is that the pairing
of Cupid and Psyche was very old, but that Apuleius may well have
invented large parts of the narrative and certainly is responsible for
the particular combination of folktale, Platonism, and literary tex-
ture that we find in his text. It is of some importance, though, how
much readers knew when they came to his version: was the story so
familiar that they knew the identity of Psyche's mysterious husband,
or was this a surprise? When they read of the oracle that pronounces
that Psyche will marry a snake, were readers fooled or is Apuleius
only pretending that they were in the dark?

Much has been made of the presence of folktales in Apuleius,
here and in the *Metamorphoses* as a whole, a topic that has generated
fierce debate (see Schlam 1992 for a good overview). Many features
of the tale belong to a fairy-tale or fable world of speaking towers and
compassionate ants that is different from the world of Lucius, magi-
cal though that world is. Structurally, the Tale involves recognizable
folktale motifs—evil sisters, a taboo against looking at or opening
something, the magical palace, the husband as monster—most of
which are documented in numerous folktales around the world, but
which are not so evident in Graeco-Roman literary texts. The im-
position of impossible labors by a more powerful figure reminds us
of stories like Rumplestiltskin (yet also of the more exalted labors of
Hercules). Certainly, Apuleius, here and elsewhere, *presents* tales as
delivered orally by non-literary figures; the current tale is narrated
by an old woman to a young girl in a robbers' den. Apuleius, then,
has fashioned the tale as deliberately sub-literary, whether it springs
from oral folktale or not. The tale also has strong literary connec-
tions—to the supernaturally beautiful heroine of Greek romance, to
Vergil's description of the Underworld, and to various episodes in
Ovid, for example, which need not be considered at odds with the
less literary features.

At the other end of the spectrum, the tale has to be read with
some awareness that Plato had written about love and the soul and
that these resonances must be of signficance in a text by a Platonic
philosopher, even if, ultimately, Apuleius is merely playing with us.
We may think in particular of the Platonic process by which the soul,

through Love, comes in contact with the divine (see above). Kenney takes another Platonic approach: "Pausanias in Plato's Symposium had distinguished two Aphrodites, Urania (Heavenly, *Venus Caelestis*) and Pandemos (Of the People, *Venus Vulgaris*) and two Eroses to correspond, their respective provinces being love of souls and bodies" (Kenney 1990, 19). These "dichotomous deities" then contend for Psyche, who represents the human soul. In the end it is the higher Cupid who wins the battle and the lower Venus who loses. The higher Venus and the lower Cupid are shadow figures, but this fundamental struggle, Kenney argues, is what the tale is really about. Relihan (2009) instead presents for us the Platonic materials that the reader would have known, asking what features would confuse them. Plato, for example, imagines the transformative love he describes as the love of boys, non-procreative love with abstract "offspring" which are explicitly defined as preferable to physical children. Apuleius has used the figures of Love and Soul, but inserted them into an emphatically heterosexual context. Is there something about this substitution that subverts the Platonic allegory from the beginning? (Relihan 2009 provides a useful and innovative introduction for the student.) Critics agree that Apuleius is engaging in an astounding enterprise by integrating folklore and Platonism, but there is little agreement on how to read that combination.

The main question about this tale, finally, is why Apuleius chose to include such a long interlude, and why this particular one. The embedded tales in the *Metamorphoses* always involve a break in the narrative and a window into a whole different world, but most are fairly brief. They relate in some way, sometimes oblique, to the frame narrative (i.e., the narrative of Lucius). In the first two and a half books, the inserted or embedded tales tell of magic and its dangers, and function as unheeded warnings to Lucius that he needs to beware of witches rather than court them. The later books contain many stories about violent, destructive characters (Thrasyllus of Book 8 or the rich landowner of Book 9) or adulterers (much of Book 9) or evil stepmothers (Book 10) that seem completely unrelated to Lucius' immediate situation. Apart from providing entertainment in themselves, these seem mainly designed to mark the world as increasingly dark and out of control; the tales chart a deteriorating world mirroring Lucius' own worsening situation as he passes from one cruel or needy owner to another and seems always further from redemption. (See further Shumate 1999.) There are clear parallels between Lucius' story and that of Psyche; both of them start out as young naive elites, leave home or are expelled, undergo a change in status through *curiositas* (Psyche by looking at Cupid and Lucius by dabbling in magic), wander and suffer as a consequence, and both finally are elevated to a higher status closer to the divine (Psyche is deified while Lucius has direct contact with Isis and becomes a priest of the cult).

An interlude, perhaps: like the tale of Lucius, Psyche's story has a slave subtext. When she disobeys the injunction against looking at Cupid, Psyche is forced to be the slave of Venus. She is repeatedly referred to as "*ancilla*" (a female house-slave), is whipped and insulted, and forced to do impossible work. Because of her beauty, she is eventually married to her master and elevated to a higher social position. The tale, told by a slave, may represent a common slave fantasy of being lifted out of slavery.

Most readers see Psyche as a mirror-image of Lucius and as a sign to the reader of what is to come for him, a comforting sign for Lucius of how his adventures will end. (The tale is more immediately designed for Charite, for whom it seems to portend a good end; after separation from her husband and various trials, she will be reunited with him. This turns out to be true initially, but her tale takes a bad turn and everyone dies.) Penwill (1975) has argued that the tale is a debased version of Lucius' adventures, where the Olympian gods, particularly Venus, are exposed as selfish and vindictive in contrast with Isis who stands above human conflict. The birth of Voluptas at the end of the tale, Penwill argues, must be read in the context of the sensual pleasure that has marked the episode, rather than as a divine joy of the sort that Lucius experiences in Book 11. This reading obviously is at odds with the kind of Platonic interpretation discussed above. Those who take a satiric view of the ending of the novel (see above), must either accept Penwill's reading of a debased "Cupid and Psyche" or read the mirror in the opposite way: Psyche is the one who achieves deification, while Lucius is deluded into thinking that he has undergone a religious revelation.

Another way of approaching these questions is to note a qualitative difference in the kinds of lives that Psyche and Lucius will henceforth lead. Whether the ending is "serious" or not, Lucius is clearly embarking on a different kind of life, a life including renunciation (of hair and meat and material goods, at least intermittently) and a life in which religious devotion plays a significant role, while Psyche has settled for what we might see as a "suburban" life, marrying and raising her child, being assimilated to the social class of her husband, living in a nice house. (Cupid, too, is described by Jupiter as now grown up enough to stop causing havoc among married couples and needing to settle down with a wife.) The contrast the episode sets up, then, highlights Lucius' choice of the spiritual life. It does not necessarily condemn the life of the ordinary citizen choosing a life at home with children; the sensuality in Cupid and Psyche's lives does not seem extreme and culpable, but rather belongs to the kind of life that Charite, for example, will live. It is paradoxical that such a life is lived in the heavens, and that the two characters have symbolic names, but when is Apuleius not paradoxical?

∾ *Isis*

As noted above, in Book 11 Lucius encounters Isis and becomes her devotee and a priest called a "pastophor" (see notes to 11.30.4). We may wonder about two issues here: first of all, is it surprising that Lucius, a Greek, should encounter and become an initiate of an Egyptian goddess or that Apuleius, writing within the Latin tradition including all the familiar Olympian gods, would introduce Isis as the culmination of the book? Secondly, Isis is referred to as the *numen unicum* and the *deorum dearumque facies uniformis*; in other words, there is a surprisingly monotheistic (or henotheistic, see below) tenor to the claims about her godhead.

Isis is, in origin, an Egyptian goddess, but her worship spread throughout Greece and later Rome in the Hellenistic Age. In part, the diffusion occurred through traders, in part through the conquest of Egypt by Alexander the Great, who had so often embraced the indigenous customs of the peoples he conquered. Isis' form and functions underwent changes as she was partially Hellenized and Romanized, so that, while she was a relatively minor deity in the Egyptian pantheon, she became a savior goddess among Greeks and Romans in the Hellenistic Age. At the same time, a new deity based on Osiris—Sarapis—was consciously created to appeal to Greeks. The Egyptian gods became part Greek, part Egyptian. One feature of this "syncretism" is the statuary of Isis; by Apuleius' time, she was typically represented like a Graeco-Roman goddess but bearing the paraphernalia of Egyptian cult—the *sistrum* (a rattle) and *situla* (pail), an Isis-knot in her tunic and a lotus flower on her head. She had a temple in Athens as early as the third century BCE and a large sanctuary in Rome that may date to the Augustan era, as well as temples spread widely throughout the Greek and Roman world. In some senses, then, she had become a deity at home among the Greeks and Romans and was to a degree assimilated with existing goddesses, especially Demeter.

In Rome, however, there was initially some resistance; her cult was formally suppressed in the late Republic, but in 43 BCE the triumvirs vowed a shrine to the goddess and the cult was made official by Caligula. Still, from the late first century CE on, much of the appeal of the cult was its foreignness and exotic nature. Rome was, in general, both fascinated and repelled by things Egyptian, and Apuleius clearly goes out of his way to emphasize its exotic nature (mostly in passages not included here). The strangeness of animal gods, indecipherable hieroglyphs, the Nile and its overflowing waters, the pyramid and shiny obelisk, exotic animals like the crocodile—all these were alluring to Romans, and to pretend that Isis and Sarapis had become domesticated into merely another set of Roman gods is to miss the nature of their strong appeal.

The cult of Isis should perhaps be understood in the context of other "mystery cults" brought in from abroad and involving a different kind of personal involvement and allegiance from what we associate with the Olympian pantheon. It used to be standard to talk of "eastern religions" and "mystery cults" that led the way to the rise of Christianity, cults that included that of Mithras, the Iranian god popular among soldiers, and Cybele, the Phrygian mother goddess who demands castration of Attis in Catullus 63. These elective cults and their practices used to be viewed in contrast with the worship of the Olympian pantheon, which had seemed merely official and obligatory and empty of spiritual feeling and personal involvement. It is now pointed out that several of these cults—the Eleusinian mysteries and the cult of Dionysus, for example—are not eastern at all and that many of the features that had been defined as either "eastern" or late had already existed. The divide between official religion and devotion taken up voluntarily for personal spiritual advancement has certainly been exaggerated, but when one reads Lucius' prayer to Isis and her response to him, one senses something rather different from Chryses' prayer to Apollo in *Iliad* 1, for example, and something more familiar to us from the traditions of Judeo-Christian spirituality. It is certainly not accidental that this is the age in which Christianity is spreading from the east to the west. For whatever reasons (not necessarily the anxiety of the age), a stronger attachment to a deity who seems to care about mortals is becoming popular. (See further Burkert 1987 and Beard, North, Price 1998.)

As for Isis' claims to be the one deity that encompasses all other deities, this, too, is at least in part a phenomenon of the age. We should read carefully what Isis says about herself at 11.5: she does not deny the existence of other deities, but rather claims that they are part of her. She includes Venus, Proserpina *and* all the gods (masculine and feminine) as well. Yet she is also careful to say that Isis is her true name and that there are right and wrong rituals with which to worship her. The claim that there is one god or goddess which includes others is sometimes referred to as "henotheism," to distinguish it from monotheism, which tends more strongly to exclude and deny the validity of other deities. Before the imperial era, in a polytheistic system, adherents tended merely to add new gods to their pantheon rather than to claim either that any new god is *the* one god or that this god subsumes all others. But Mithras and Isis and perhaps others, who have become popular under the Empire, tend to command a different kind of personal connection and allegiance, which grows in popularity among the general population. We should not underestimate the religious awe and fervor of earlier religion, nor the individual attachment to particular gods (e.g., Odysseus and Athena). Still, we are seeing something rather new in the description of Isis as the one face of all gods and goddesses and in Lucius' almost obsessive devotion to her. How exactly this squares with the introduction of two new Egyptian deities in the last few sections is quite problematic; see above.

∾ *Style*

One of the first things the advanced student notices reading Apuleius is that his style is utterly different from the prose style of Cicero, Sallust, or Livy. He is fond of rhyme, alliteration, and rhythmical clausulae of this sort: *saeva scaeva, virosa ebriosa, pervicax pertinax, in rapinis turpibus avara, in sumptibus foedis profusa . . .* ("cruel and perverse, crazy for men and wine, headstrong and obstinate, grasping in her mean thefts and a spendthrift in her loathsome extravagances," 9.14, a passage describing a vile woman who, incidentally, worshipped only one god). It is a baroque, exuberant style striving above all for richness and even excess, full of rhetorical devices and tropes drawn from his practice as a rhetorician. Sometimes this incantatory style can seem to relate to the central theme of magic in the book; in certain passages, such as the description of Cupid at 5.22 or that on slaves at 9.12–13, Apuleius employs these devices full force because the extraordinary subject-matter demands new modes of expression, but his ornateness is not reserved for extraordinary circumstances.

    Apuleius is difficult to translate, but usually not because his sentences are long and periodic like those of Cicero. In fact, he prefers parataxis to hypotaxis (subordination). Rather, it is his inventiveness in vocabulary, his twisting of the meanings of words, his love of periphrasis and deliberate creation of ambiguity that make him, at times, difficult. Compiling the total vocabulary for this book, I was struck by how many words in the text are *hapax legomena* and how often Apuleius departs from the standard meaning of a word in the *Oxford Latin Dictionary*. He is fond of changing the genders of words (as in 1.1 where he has made Mt. Hymettus feminine) and he recuperates archaic vocabulary from Plautus and other comic poets in particular—which was something of a vogue in his age.

Apuleius' Latin looks different in part because he lived and worked in the second century CE, two centuries after Cicero or Vergil. Like any language, Latin was changing and shows some incipient Romance language features; for example, *ille* and *illa*, which become articles in French, Italian, and Spanish, show some signs of moving in that direction at, for example, 4.4.1, *illi latrones* (see commentary). Sometimes *quod* with the subjunctive is used to introduce indirect discourse in place of the infinitive with accusative construction of Classical Latin, as at 4.5.6: . . . *conloquentes quod esset . . . sedes illa et habitatio* ("saying that there was their home and domicile"). Some of these anomalous structures are a feature of the era, and some may be due to Apuleius' efforts to create the appearance, at times, of a vernacular tone, an oral mode of writing. It used to be claimed that Apuleius' style was a matter of "*Africitas*," a different style or dialect associated with the fact that Apuleius is from North Africa. This argument was refuted by scholars who pointed out that any given linguistic peculiarity of Apuleius' style is always attested elsewhere in Italian Latin, and that many of the striking features of Apuleius' style—archaizing, for example—are a feature of later Latin, attested in other contemporary writers. Nonetheless, the sheer abundance of these features in Apuleius is remarkable and it is possible, and has been argued, that this style could be associated with rhetorical schools of Carthage. When we consider the exceptional nature of his style, then, we should keep in mind that it is later than Latin we normally read and that it was composed in a different geographical region by a writer who was also surrounded by speakers of African languages and who, in general, liked to shake up the status quo. A good introduction to Apuleius' style may be found in E. J. Kenney's commentary on Cupid and Psyche, pp. 28–38.

∾ The later "reception" of Apuleius

While Apuleius is not as well known today as some other Classical authors, he was extremely popular in the Renaissance. Boccaccio transcribed some of the works of Apuleius and borrowed several of the adultery tales for the *Decameron*. He also created an "allegory of Psyche" in another work. Shakespeare was influenced by Apuleius via the Adlington translation of 1566; most obviously, Bottom's partial transformation into an ass in *A Midsummer Night's Dream* is a clear reworking of Lucius' metamorphosis. Several Renaissance fresco cycles illustrate the tale of Cupid and Psyche (Raphael at the Villa Farnesina, 1518; Guilio Romano in Mantua, 1520s). One might also mention C. S. Lewis' *Till We have Faces* (1956), which rewrites *Cupid and Psyche* as a Christian allegory. There is much more. Julia Haig Gaisser and Robert Carver have recently documented the rich afterlife of Apuleius' works in complementary ways.

∾ Manuscripts

The only manuscript that will be mentioned in this commentary is the eleventh-century Codex Laurentianus 68.2, known as F, from which it is believed that all the other existing manuscripts of Apuleius are derived. Also important is Codex Laurentianus 29.2 or φ of the twelfth or thirteenth century which was copied from F and is used in cases where F is illegible.

∾ Suggested readings

Beard, M., J. North, and S. Price. *Religions of Rome*, 2 vols. Cambridge: Cambridge University Press, 1998.

Bitel, A. "Quis ille Asinus aureus? The Metamorphoses of Apuleius' Title." *Ancient Narrative* 1 (2000–2001): 208–44.

Bowie, E. "The Chronology of the earlier Greek novels since B. E. Perry: revisions and precisions." *Ancient Narrative* 2 (2002): 47–63.

Bradley, K. *Apuleius and Antonine Rome: Historical Essays*, Toronto: University of Toronto Press, 2012.

———. "Apuleius and Carthage." *Ancient Narrative* 4 (2005): 1–29.

———. "Animalizing the Slave: the truth of fiction." *Journal of Roman Studies* 90 (2000): 110–25.

Burkert, W. *Ancient Mystery Cults.* Cambridge, MA: Harvard University Press, 1987.

———. *Lore and Science in Ancient Pythagoreanism.* Cambridge, MA: Harvard University Press, 1972.

Callebat, L. *Sermo Cotidianus dans les Métamorphoses d'Apulée.* Caen: Faculté des lettres et sciences, Caen, 1968.

Carver, Robert. *The Protean Ass: the Metamorphoses of Apuleius from Antiquity to the Renaissance.* Oxford: Oxford University Press, 2008.

Dillon, J. *The Middle Platonists.* Second edition. Ithaca, NY: Cornell University Press, 1996.

Doody, M. *The True Story of the Novel.* New Brunswick, NJ: Rutgers University Press, 1996.

Drews, F. "Asinus Philosophans: Allegory's *Fate* and Isis' *Providence* in the *Metamorphoses*." In *Aspects of Apuleius' Golden Ass, Volume III: The Isis Book, A Collection of Original Papers,* edited by Wytse Keulen and Ulrike Egelhaaf-Gaiser, 107–131. Leiden: Brill, 2012.

Egelhaaf-Gaiser, Ulrike. "The Gleaming Pate of the *Pastophorus*." In Keulen and Egelhaaf-Gaiser, 42–72. Leiden: Brill, 2012.

Finkelpearl, E. *Metamophosis of Language in Apuleius: a study of allusion in the novel.* Ann Arbor: University of Michigan Press, 1998.

———. "Apuleius, the *Onos* and Rome." In *The Greek and Roman Novel: Parallel Readings,* 263–76. Ancient Narrative Supplementum 8. Groningen: Barkhuis Publishing, 2007.

———. "Marsyas the Satyr and Apuleius of Madauros." *Ramus* 38.1 (2009): 7–42.

Fitzgerald, W. *Slavery and the Roman Literary Imagination.* Cambridge: Cambridge University Press, 2000.

Fredouille, J-C. *Apulée Metamorphoseon Liber XI*. Paris: Presses Universitaires de France, 1975.

Gaisser, J. *The Fortunes of Apuleius and the Golden Ass, A Study in Transmission and Reception*. Princeton: Princeton University Press, 2008.

Gollnick, J. *Love and the Soul: Psychological Interpretations of the Eros and Psyche Myth*. Waterloo (Ontario): Wilfrid Laurier University Press, 1992.

Graverini, L. "Prudentia and Providentia: Book XI in context." In Keulen and Egelhaaf-Gaiser, 86–106.

Griffiths, J. G. *Apuleius of Madauros, The Isis-Book*. Leiden: Brill, 1977.

Hall, E. "The Ass with Double Vision: Politicising an Ancient Greek Novel." In *Heart of the Heartless World: Essays in Cultural Resistance in Memory of Margot Heinemann*, edited by D. Margoulis and M. Joannou, 47–59. London and Boulder, CO: Pluto Press, 1995.

Hanson, J. A. *Apuleius Metamorphoses*. Two volumes. Loeb Classical Library. Cambridge: Harvard University Press, 1989.

Harrison, S. J. "*Apuleius'* Metamorphoses." In *The Novel in the Ancient World*, edited by G. Schmeling, 491–516. Leiden: Brill, 1996.

———. *Apuleius, A Latin Sophist*. Oxford: Oxford University Press, 2000.

———. *Apuleius Rhetorical Works*. Translated by J. L. Hilton and V. J. C. Hunink. Oxford: Oxford University Press, 2001.

Hijmans, B. L., R. Th. van der Paardt, E. R. Smits, R. E. H. Westendorp Boerma, and A. G. Westerbrink. *Apuleius Madaurensis Metamorphoses Book IV 1-27, Text, Introduction and Commentary*. Groningen: Bouma's Boekhuis, 1977.

Hijmans, B. L., R. Th. van der Paardt, V. Schmidt, B. Wesseling, and M. Zimmerman. *Apuleius Madaurensis Metamorphoses, Book IX, Text, Introduction and Commentary*. Groningen: Egbert Forsten, 1995.

Hofmann, H., ed. *Latin Fiction: The Latin Novel in Context*. New York: Routledge, 1999.

Kahane, A., and A. Laird, eds. *A Companion to the Prologue to Apuleius' Metamorphoses*. Oxford: Oxford University Press, 2001.

Kenney, E. *Apuleius, Cupid and Psyche*. Cambridge: Cambridge University Press, 1990.

———. "In the Mill with Slaves: Lucius Looks Back in Gratitude." *Transactions and Proceedings of the American Philological Association* 133 (2003): 159–92.

Keulen, W. *Apuleius Metamorphoses* I. Groningen: Egbert Forsten, 2006.

Keulen, W., and U. Egelhaaf-Gaiser. *Aspects of Apuleius' Golden Ass, Volume III: The Isis Book, A Collection of Original Papers*. Leiden: Brill 2012.

Penwill, J. "Slavish Pleasures and Profitless Curiosity: Fall and Redemption in Apuleius' *Metamorphoses*." *Ramus* 4 (1975): 49–82.

———. "*Ambages Reciprocae*: Reviewing Apuleius' *Metamorphoses*." In *The Imperial Muse: Flavian Epicists to Claudian*, edited by A. J. Boyle, 211–35. Ramus essays on Roman literature and the Empire. Victoria, Australia: Aureal Publications, 1990.

Reardon, B. P. *Collected Ancient Greek Novels*. Berkeley and Los Angeles: University of California Press, 1989.

Relihan, J., trans. *Apuleius, The Tale of Cupid and Psyche*. Indianapolis and Cambridge, MA: Hackett Publishing Co., 2009.

Ruebel, J. *Apuleius, The Metamorphoses Book I*. Wauconda, IL: Bolchazy-Carducci, 2000.

Sandy, G. N. *The Greek World of Apuleius: Apuleius and the Second Sophistic*. Leiden: Brill, 1997.

Schlam, C. *Cupid and Psyche: Apuleius and the Monuments*. University Park, PA: The American Philological Association, 1976.

———. *The Metamorphoses of Apuleius: On Making an Ass of Oneself*. Chapel Hill: University of North Carolina Press, 1992.

Schmeling, G., ed. *The Novel in the Ancient World*. Leiden: Brill, 1996.

Shumate, N. *Crisis and Conversion in Apuleius' Metamorphoses*. Ann Arbor: University of Michigan Press, 1996.

——. "Apuleius' Metamorphoses, the inserted tales." In *Latin Fiction, the Latin Novel in Context*, edited by Heinz Hofmann, 113–125. London and New York: Routledge, 1999.

Takács, S. *Isis and Sarapis in the Roman World*. Leiden: Brill, 1995.

Tilg, S. "Lucius on Poetics? The Prologue to Apuleius' *Metamorphoses* Reconsidered." *Studi italiani di filologia classica* 5.2 (2007): 156–98.

Turpin, W. *Apuleius Metamorphoses Book III*. Bryn Mawr, PA: Bryn Mawr Latin Commentaries, 2002.

van der Paardt, R. Th. *L. Apuleius Madaurensis, The Metamorphoses, A commentary on book III with text and introduction*. Amsterdam: Hakkert, 1971.

van Mal-Maeder, D. "Lector intende: laetaberis. The Enigma of the Last Book of Apuleius' *Metamorphoses*." In *Groningen Colloquia on the Novel* 8 (1997): 87–118.

Whitmarsh, T. *Greek Literature and the Roman Empire. The Politics of Imitation*. Oxford: Oxford University Press, 1999.

Winkler, J. J. *Auctor and Actor: A Narratological Reading of Apuleius's The Golden Ass*. Berkeley and Los Angeles: University of California Press, 1985.

Witt, R. E. *Isis in the Graeco-Roman World*. Ithaca, NY: Cornell University Press, 1971.

Zimmerman, M. *Apuleius Madaurensis Metamorphoses Book X*. Groningen: Egbert Forsten, 2000.

Zimmerman, M., S. Panayotakis, V. C. Hunink, W. H. Keulen, S. J. Harrison, Th. D. McCreight, B. Wesseling, and D. van Mal-Maeder. *Apuleius Madaurensis, Metamorphoses Books IV 28–35, V and VI 1–24, the Tale of Cupid and Psyche*. Groningen: Egbert Forsten, 2004.

Latin Text

The text used in this edition is that of Rudolf Helm, *Apuleius I, Metamorphoseon Libri XI*, Leipzig: Teubner, 1968, with the exception of the words and phrases below.

I have changed consonantal *u* of Helm to *v* because this orthography is usually more familiar to students. I have also sometimes changed punctuation for clarity, generally isolating more phrases. My text dispenses with the brackets and carats of Helm, following his emendations, but leaving out the orthographical marks, for greater readability.

I have, however, used the numbering system from the edition of D. S. Robertson, *Apulée, Les Métamorphoses,* Paris: Les Belles Lettres, Collection Budé, 1956.

∾ *Divergences from Teubner text of Helm*

2.6.5 ex voto diutino Helm; et voto diutino Robertson

2.6.6 enim vero Helm; enimvero Robertson

2.7.2 [ambacu pascuae iurulenta] Helm; †ambacu pascuae† iurulenta van Mal-Maeder (GCA)

3.1.2 vesper<ti>ni Helm; vesperni F, van der Paardt

3.2.1 turbae miscellaneae <frequentia> Helm; turbae miscellaneae F

3.2.4 circumse<cus va>dentis Helm; circumfluentis Pricaeus, Robertson

3.9.6 luctantem Helm; reluctantem Robertson, φ

3.10.1 graculari Helm; gratulari F

3.22.1 magicis Helm; magnis F

4.5.2 in <modum> mortui Helm; in mortuum F (later correction), Hanson

4.28.3 pri<m>ore digito Helm; priore digito F, GCA

4.28.3 <ea>m ut ipsam Helm; ut ipsam, Robertson

4.29.3 proferuntur Helm; proteruntur Robertson

4.29.4 frequenter Helm, F; frequentes, Robertson

4.30.3 faxo <eam> Helm; faxo F, GCA

5.22.7 faretra Helm; pharetra Robertson

6.24.3 . . . . . Apollo, Helm; Apollo (no ellipsis) Robertson, Kenney

6.24.3 <aut> tibias inflarent, Saturus Helm; tibias inflaret Saturus, F., Robertson

6.24.3 dicerent Helm, F; diceret Robertson

10.16.9 clamor Helm; et clamor F, Robertson, GCA

11.5.4 [omitte] Helm; omitte F, Robertson

11.30.4 quae, Helm; quam F, Fredouille

11. 30. 4 ibide[serui]<m sustin>ebat, Helm; ibidem exciuerat Robertson

11.30.4 pastoforum F, Helm; pastophorum Robertson

11.30.5 qua<m> raso, Helm; quaqua raso, Robertson

◆ *METAMORPHOSES*

Book 1

1.1.1–1.2.1

1.1 At ego tibi sermone isto Milesio varias fabulas   1

conseram auresque tuas benivolas lepido susurro

permulceam—modo si papyrum Aegyptiam argutia

Nilotici calami inscriptam non spreveris inspicere—,

5   figuras fortunasque hominum in alias imagines   2

conversas et in se rursum mutuo nexu refectas ut mireris.

exordior. quis ille? paucis accipe. Hymettos Attica et   3

Isthmos Ephyrea et Taenaros Spartiaca, glebae felices

aeternum libris felicioribus conditae, mea vetus prosapia

10 est; ibi linguam Attidem primis pueritiae stipendiis   4

merui. mox in urbe Latia advena studiorum Quiritium

indigenam sermonem aerumnabili labore, nullo

magistro praeeunte, aggressus excolui. en ecce   5

praefamur veniam, siquid exotici ac forensis sermonis

15 rudis locutor offendero. iam haec equidem ipsa vocis   6

immutatio desultoriae scientiae stilo quem accessimus

respondet. fabulam Graecanicam incipimus. lector

intende: laetaberis.

1.2 Thessaliam — nam et illic originis maternae nostrae   1

20 fundamenta a Plutarcho illo inclito ac mox Sexto

philosopho nepote eius prodita gloriam nobis faciunt—

eam Thessaliam ex negotio petebam.

Book 2
2.1.1–2.2.1

2.1 Ut primum nocte discussa sol novus diem fecit, et   1
somno simul emersus et lectulo, anxius alioquin et
nimis cupidus cognoscendi quae rara miraque sunt,
reputansque me media Thessaliae loca tenere, qua artis   2
5 magicae nativa cantamina totius orbis consono ore
celebrentur, fabulamque illam optimi comitis
Aristomenis de situ civitatis huius exortam, suspensus
alioquin et voto simul et studio, curiose singula
considerabam. nec fuit in illa civitate quod aspiciens id   3
10 esse crederem quod esset, sed omnia prorsus ferali
murmure in aliam effigiem translata, ut et lapides quos   4
offenderem de homine duratos et aves quas audirem
indidem plumatas, et arbores quae pomerium ambirent
similiter foliatas, et fontanos latices de corporibus
15 humanis fluxos crederem. iam statuas et imagines   5
incessuras, parietes locuturos, boves et id genus pecua
dicturas praesagium, de ipso vero caelo et iubaris orbe
subito venturum oraculum.

2.2 Sic attonitus, immo vero cruciabili desiderio   1
20 stupidus, nullo quidem initio vel omnino vestigio
cupidinis meae reperto, cuncta circumibam tamen.

2.6–7

2.6 At ego curiosus alioquin, ut primum artis magicae   1
semper optatum nomen audivi, tantum a cautela
Pamphiles afui ut etiam ultro gestirem tali magisterio   2
me volens ampla cum mercede tradere et prorsus in
5 ipsum barathrum saltu concito praecipitare. festinus   3
denique et vecors animi manu eius velut catena quadam
memet expedio et "salve" propere addito ad Milonis
hospitium perniciter evolo. ac dum amenti similis celero   4
vestigium, "age," inquam, "o Luci, evigila et tecum esto.
10 habes exoptatam occasionem, et voto diutino poteris   5
fabulis miris explere pectus. aufer formidines pueriles,   6
comminus cum re ipsa naviter congredere, et a nexu
quidem venerio hospitis tuae tempera, et probi Milonis
genialem torum religiosus suspice, verum enimvero Fotis
15 famula petatur enixe. nam et forma scitula et moribus   7
ludicra et prorsus argutula est. vesperi quoque cum
somno concederes, et in cubiculum te deduxit comiter et
blande lectulo collocavit et satis amanter cooperuit et
osculato tuo capite, quam invita discederet vultu
20 prodidit, denique saepe retrorsa respiciens substitit.
quod bonum felix et faustum itaque, licet salutare non   8
erit, Photis illa temptetur."

2.7 Haec mecum ipse disputans fores Milonis accedo et,   1
quod aiunt, pedibus in sententiam meam vado. nec
25 tamen domi Milonem vel uxorem eius offendo, sed

tantum caram meam Fotidem: suis parabat viscum   2

fartim concisum et pulpam frustatim consectam

†ambacu pascuae† iurulenta et, quod naribus iam inde

ariolabar, tuccetum perquam sapidissimum. ipsa linea   3

30   tunica mundule amicta et russea fasceola praenitente

altiuscule sub ipsas papillas succinctula, illud cibarium

vasculum floridis palmulis rotabat in circulum, et in

orbis flexibus crebra succutiens et simul membra sua

leniter inlubricans, lumbis sensim vibrantibus, spinam

35   mobilem quatiens placide decenter undabat. isto aspectu   4

defixus obstupui et mirabundus steti, steterunt et

membra quae iacebant ante. et tandem ad illam: "quam   5

pulchre quamque festive," inquam "Fotis mea, ollulam

istam cum natibus intorques! quam mellitum pulmentum   6

40   apparas! felix et certo certius beatus cui permiseris illuc

digitum intingere." Tunc illa lepida alioquin et dicacula   7

puella: "discede,"inquit "miselle, quam procul a meo

foculo, discede. nam si te vel modice meus igniculus

afflaverit, ureris intime nec ullus extinguet ardorem

45   tuum nisi ego, quae dulce condiens et ollam et lectulum

suave quatere novi."

Book 3
3.1.1–3.2.5

3.1 Commodum punicantibus phaleris Aurora roseum   1
quatiens lacertum caelum inequitabat, et me securae
quieti revulsum nox diei reddidit. aestus invadit animum   2
vesperni recordatione facinoris; complicitis denique
5   pedibus ac palmulis in alternas digitorum vicissitudines
super genua conexis, sic grabattum cossim insidens
ubertim flebam, iam forum et iudicia, iam sententiam,
ipsum denique carnificem imaginabundus. "an mihi   3
quisquam tam mitis tamque benivolus iudex obtinget,
10   qui me trinae caedis cruore perlitum et tot civium
sanguine delibutum innocentem pronuntiare poterit?
hanc illam mihi gloriosam peregrinationem fore   4
Chaldaeus Diophanes obstinate praedicabat." haec   5
identidem mecum replicans fortunas meas heiulabam.
15   quati fores interdum et frequenti clamore ianuae nostrae
perstrepi.

3.2 nec mora, cum magna inruptione patefactis aedibus,   1
magistratibus eorumque ministris et turbae miscellaneae
cuncta completa statimque lictores duo de iussu
20   magistratuum immissa manu trahere me sane non
renitentem occipiunt. ac dum primum angiportum   2
insistimus, statim civitas omnis in publicum effusa mira
densitate nos insequitur. et quamquam capite in terram   3
immo ad ipsos inferos iam deiecto maestus incederem,
25   obliquato tamen aspectu rem admirationis maximae

conspicio: nam inter tot milia populi circumfluentis 4

nemo prorsum qui non risu dirumperetur aderat.

3.2.7–9

3.2 nec mora, cum passim populus procurrens caveae 7

conseptum mira celeritate complevit; aditus etiam et 8

tectum omne fartim stipaverant, plerique columnis

implexi, alii statuis dependuli, nonnulli per fenestras et

5 lacunaria semiconspicui, miro tamen omnes studio

visendi pericula salutis neclegebant. tunc me per 9

proscaenium medium velut quandam victimam publica

ministeria producunt et orchestrae mediae sistunt.

3.8.1–4

3.8 Inter haec quaedam mulier per medium theatrum 1

lacrimosa et flebilis atra veste contecta parvulum

quendam sinu tolerans decurrit ac pone eam anus alia

pannis horridis obsita paribusque maesta fletibus, ramos

5 oleagineos utraeque quatientes, quae circumfusae 2

lectulum, quo peremptorum cadavera contecta fuerant,

plangore sublato se lugubriter eiulantes: "per publicam 3

misericordiam, per commune ius humanitatis," aiunt,

"miseremini indigne caesorum iuvenum nostraeque

10 viduitati ac solitudini de vindicta solacium date. certe 4

parvuli huius in primis annis destituti fortunis succurrite

et de latronis huius sanguine legibus vestris et disciplinae

publicae litate."

3.9.5–3.11.6

3.9 His dictis adplauditur et ilico me magistratus ipsum 5
iubet corpora, quae lectulo fuerant posita, mea manu
detegere. reluctantem me ac diu rennuentem praecedens 6
facinus instaurare nova ostensione, lictores iussu
5　magistratuum, quam instantissime compellunt, manum
denique ipsam e regione lateris trudentes in exitium suum
super ipsa cadavera porrigunt. evictus tandem necessitate 7
succumbo, et, ingratis licet, abrepto pallio retexi corpora.
dii boni, quae facies rei? quod monstrum? quae
10　fortunarum mearum repentina mutatio? quamquam 8
enim iam in peculio Proserpinae et Orci familia
numeratus, subito in contrariam faciem obstupefactus
haesi, nec possum novae illius imaginis rationem idoneis
verbis expedire. nam cadavera illa iugulatorum hominum 9
15　erant tres utres inflati variisque secti foraminibus et, ut
vespertinum proelium meum recordabar, his locis hiantes,
quibus latrones illos vulneraveram.

3.10 Tunc ille quorundam astu paulisper cohibitus risus 1
libere iam exarsit in plebem. hi gaudii nimietate gratulari,
20　illi dolorem ventris manuum compressione sedare. et
certe laetitia delibuti meque respectantes cuncti theatro
facessunt. at ego, ut primum illam laciniam prenderam, 2
fixus in lapidem steti gelidus nihil secus quam una de
ceteris theatri statuis vel columnis. nec prius ab inferis 3
25　emersi quam Milon hospes accessit et iniecta manu me
renitentem lacrimisque rursum promicantibus crebra
singultientem clementi violentia secum adtraxit, et 4

observatis viae solitudinibus per quosdam amfractus
domum suam perduxit, maestumque me atque etiam
30 tunc trepidum variis solatur affatibus. nec tamen   5
indignationem iniuriae, quae inhaeserat altius meo
pectori, ullo modo permulcere quivit.

3.11 Ecce ilico etiam ipsi magistratus cum suis insignibus   1
domum nostram ingressi talibus me monitis delenire
35 gestiunt: "neque tuae dignitatis vel etiam prosapiae
tuorum ignari sumus, Luci domine; nam et provinciam
totam inclitae vestrae familiae nobilitas conplectitur. ac   2
ne istud quod vehementer ingemescis contumeliae causa
perpessus es. omnem itaque de tuo pectore praesentem
40 tristitudinem mitte et angorem animi depelle. nam lusus   3
iste, quem publice gratissimo deo Risui per annua
reverticula sollemniter celebramus, semper commenti
novitate florescit. iste deus auctorem et actorem suum   4
propitius ubique comitabitur amanter nec umquam
45 patietur ut ex animo doleas sed frontem tuam serena
venustate laetabit adsidue. at tibi civitas omnis pro ista   5
gratia honores egregios obtulit; nam et patronum scribsit
et ut in aere stet imago tua decrevit." ad haec dicta   6
sermonis vicem refero: "tibi quidem," inquam
50 "splendidissima et unica Thessaliae civitas, honorum
talium parem gratiam memini, verum statuas et imagines
dignioribus meique maioribus reservare suadeo."

3.21.1–3.22.5

3.21 Ad hunc modum transactis voluptarie paucis   1
noctibus, quadam die percita Fotis ac satis trepida me
accurrit indicatque dominam suam, quod nihil etiam
tunc in suos amores ceteris artibus promoveret, nocte
5 proxima in avem sese plumaturam atque ad suum
cupitum sic devolaturam; proin memet ad rei tantae   2
speculam caute praepararem. iamque circa primam   3
noctis vigiliam ad illud superius cubiculum suspenso et
insono vestigio me perducit ipsa perque rimam ostiorum
10 quampiam iubet arbitrari quae sic gesta sunt. iam   4
primum omnibus laciniis se devestit Pamphile et, arcula
quadam reclusa pyxides plusculas inde depromit, de quis
unius operculo remoto atque indidem egesta unguedine
diuque palmulis suis adfricta ab imis unguibus sese
15 totam adusque summos capillos perlinit, multumque
cum lucerna secreto conlocuta, membra tremulo
succussu quatit. quis leniter fluctuantibus promicant   5
molles plumulae, crescunt et fortes pinnulae, duratur
nasus incurvus, coguntur ungues adunci. fit bubo   6
20 Pamphile. sic edito stridore querulo iam sui
periclitabunda paulatim terra resultat, mox in altum
sublimata forinsecus totis alis evolat.

3.22 Et illa quidem magnis suis artibus volens reformatur,   1
at ego, nullo decantatus carmine, praesentis tantum facti
25 stupore defixus, quidvis aliud magis videbar esse quam
Lucius: sic exterminatus animi, attonitus in amentiam   2
vigilans somniabar; defrictis adeo diu pupulis, an

vigilarem scire quaerebam. tandem denique reversus ad   3

sensum praesentium, adrepta manu Fotidis et admota

30   meis luminibus: "patere, oro te," inquam "dum dictat   4

occasio, magno et singulari me adfectionis tuae fructu

perfrui et impertire nobis unctulum indidem per istas   5

tuas papillas, mea mellitula, tuumque mancipium

inremunerabili beneficio sic tibi perpetuo pignera ac iam

35   perfice ut meae Veneri Cupido pinnatus adsistam tibi."

3.24–26

3.24 Haec identidem adseverans summa cum trepidatione   1

inrepit cubiculum et pyxidem depromit arcula. quam ego   2

amplexus ac deosculatus prius, utque mihi prosperis

faveret volatibus deprecatus, abiectis propere laciniis totis,

5   avide manus immersi et, haurito plusculo uncto, corporis

mei membra perfricui. iamque, alternis conatibus libratis   3

brachiis, in avem similem gestiebam; nec ullae plumulae

nec usquam pinnulae, sed plane pili mei crassantur in   4

setas et cutis tenella duratur in corium et in extimis

10   palmulis, perdito numero, toti digiti coguntur in singulas

ungulas, et de spinae meae termino grandis cauda

procedit. iam facies enormis et os prolixum et nares   5

hiantes et labiae pendulae; sic et aures inmodicis

horripilant auctibus. nec ullum miserae reformationis   6

15   video solacium, nisi quod mihi iam nequeunti tenere

Fotidem natura crescebat.

3.25 ac dum salutis inopia cuncta corporis mei   1

considerans, non avem me sed asinum video, querens de

facto Fotidis, sed iam humano gestu simul et voce
20   privatus, quod solum poteram, postrema deiecta labia,
umidis tamen oculis oblicum respiciens ad illam, tacitus
expostulabam. quae ubi primum me talem aspexit,   2
percussit faciem suam manibus infestis et: "occisa sum
misera:" clamavit "me trepidatio simul et festinatio fefellit,
25   et pyxidum similitudo decepit. sed bene, quod facilior   3
reformationis huius medela suppeditat. nam rosis tantum
demorsicatis exibis asinum statimque in meum Lucium
postliminio redibis. atque utinam vesperi de more nobis   4
parassem corollas aliquas, ne moram talem patereris vel
30   noctis unius. sed primo diluculo remedium festinabitur
tibi."

3.26 Sic illa maerebat, ego vero, quamquam perfectus   1
asinus et pro Lucio iumentum, sensum tamen retinebam
humanum. diu denique ac multum mecum ipse   2
35   deliberavi, an nequissimam facinerosissimamque illam
feminam spissis calcibus feriens et mordicus adpetens
necare deberem. sed ab incepto temerario melior me   3
sententia revocavit, ne morte multata Fotide salutares
mihi suppetias rursus extinguerem. deiecto itaque et   4
40   quassanti capite ac demussata temporali contumelia,
durissimo casui meo serviens, ad equum illum vectorem
meum probissimum in stabulum concedo, ubi alium
etiam Milonis quondam hospitis mei asinum stabulantem
inveni. atque ego rebar, si quod inesset mutis animalibus   5
45   tacitum ac naturale sacramentum, agnitione ac
miseratione quadam inductum, equum illum meum

hospitium ac loca lautia mihi praebiturum. sed pro   6

Iuppiter hospitalis et Fidei secreta numina! praeclarus

ille vector meus cum asino capita conferunt in meamque

50   perniciem ilico consentiunt et verentes scilicet cibariis   7

suis vix me praesepio videre proximantem: deiectis

auribus iam furentes infestis calcibus insecuntur. et   8

abigor quam procul ab ordeo, quod adposueram vesperi

meis manibus illi gratissimo famulo.

Book 4
4.4–5

4.4 Nec mora, cum iam in meridiem prono iubare   1
rursum nos ac praecipue me longe gravius onustum
producunt illi latrones stabulo. iamque confecta bona   2
parte itineris, et viae spatio defectus et sarcinae pondere
5 depressus, ictibusque fustium fatigatus, atque etiam
ungulis extritis iam claudus et titubans, rivulum   3
quendam serpentis leniter aquae propter insistens,
subtilem occasionem feliciter nactus, cogitabam totum
memet flexis scite cruribus pronum abicere, certus atque   4
10 obstinatus nullis verberibus ad ingrediundum exsurgere,
immo etiam paratus non fusti tantum sed machaera
perfossus occumbere. rebar enim iam me prorsus   5
exanimatum ac debilem mereri causariam missionem,
certe latrones partim inpatientia morae partim studio
15 festinatae fugae dorsi mei sarcinam duobus ceteris
iumentis distributuros meque in altioris vindictae vicem
lupis et vulturiis praedam relicturos.

4.5 sed tam bellum consilium meum praevertit sors   1
deterrima. namque ille alius asinus, divinato et antecapto
20 meo cogitatu, statim se mentita lassitudine cum rebus
totis offudit, iacensque in mortuum non fustibus non   2
stimulis ac ne cauda et auribus cruribusque undique
versum elevatis temptavit exsurgere, quoad tandem   3
postumae spei fatigati secumque conlocuti, ne tam diu
25 mortuo immo vero lapideo asino servientes fugam
morarentur, sarcinis eius mihi equoque distributis,   4

destricto gladio poplites eius totos amputant, ac paululum
a via retractum per altissimum praeceps in vallem
proximam etiam nunc spirantem praecipitant. tunc ego　　5
30　miseri commilitonis fortunam cogitans statui iam dolis
abiectis et fraudibus asinum me bonae frugi dominis
exhibere. nam et secum eos animadverteram　　　　6
conloquentes quod in proximo nobis esset habenda
mansio et totius viae finis quieta eorumque esset sedes
35　illa et habitatio. clementi denique transmisso clivulo　　7
pervenimus ad locum destinatum, ubi rebus totis
exsolutis atque intus conditis iam pondere liberatus
lassitudinem vice lavacri pulvereis volutatibus digerebam.

4.28.1–4.30.3

4.28 "Erant in quadam civitate rex et regina. hi tres　　1
numero filias forma conspicuas habuere, sed maiores
quidem natu, quamvis gratissima specie, idonee tamen
celebrari posse laudibus humanis credebantur. at vero　　2
5　puellae iunioris tam praecipua tam praeclara pulchritudo
nec exprimi ac ne sufficienter quidem laudari sermonis
humani penuria poterat. multi denique civium et advenae　　3
copiosi, quos eximii spectaculi rumor studiosa celebritate
congregabat, inaccessae formonsitatis admiratione
10　stupidi et admoventes oribus suis dexteram priore digito
in erectum pollicem residente ut ipsam prorsus deam
Venerem religiosis venerabantur adorationibus. iamque　　4
proximas civitates et attiguas regiones fama pervaserat
deam quam caerulum profundum pelagi peperit et ros

15 spumantium fluctuum educavit iam numinis sui passim
tributa venia in mediis conversari populi coetibus, vel
certe rursum novo caelestium stillarum germine non
maria sed terras Venerem aliam virginali flore praeditam
pullulasse.

20 **4.29** sic immensum procedit in dies opinio, sic insulas   1
iam proxumas et terrae plusculum provinciasque
plurimas fama porrecta pervagatur. iam multi mortalium   2
longis itineribus atque altissimis maris meatibus ad
saeculi specimen gloriosum confluebant. Paphon nemo   3

25 Cnidon nemo ac ne ipsa quidem Cythera ad conspectum
deae Veneris navigabant; sacra differuntur, templa
deformantur, pulvinaria proteruntur, caerimoniae
negleguntur; incoronata simulacra et arae viduae frigido
cinere foedatae. puellae supplicatur et in humanis   4

30 vultibus deae tantae numina placantur, et in matutino
progressu virginis, victimis et epulis Veneris absentis
nomen propitiatur, iamque per plateas commeantem
populi frequentes floribus sertis et solutis adprecantur.
haec honorum caelestium ad puellae mortalis cultum   5

35 inmodica translatio verae Veneris vehementer incendit
animos, et inpatiens indignationis capite quassanti
fremens altius sic secum disserit:

4.30 'en rerum naturae prisca parens, en elementorum   1
origo initialis, en orbis totius alma Venus, quae cum

40 mortali puella partiario maiestatis honore tractor et
nomen meum caelo conditum terrenis sordibus
profanatur! nimirum communi numinis piamento   2

vicariae venerationis incertum sustinebo et imaginem

meam circumferet puella moritura. frustra me pastor ille   3

45   cuius iustitiam fidemque magnus comprobavit Iuppiter

ob eximiam speciem tantis praetulit deabus. sed non

adeo gaudens ista, quaecumque est, meos honores

usurpabit: iam faxo huius etiam ipsius inlicitae

formonsitatis paeniteat.'

Book 5
5.11.3–4

5.11 Interea Psychen maritus ille quem nescit rursum   3
suis illis nocturnis sermonibus sic commonet: 'videsne
quantum tibi periculum? velitatur Fortuna eminus, ac
nisi longe firmiter praecaves, mox comminus
5   congredietur. perfidae lupulae magnis conatibus nefarias   4
insidias tibi comparant, quarum summa est ut te
suadeant meos explorare vultus, quos, ut tibi saepe
praedixi, non videbis si videris.'

5.22–23

5.22 tunc Psyche et corporis et animi alioquin infirma   1
fati tamen saevitia subministrante viribus roboratur, et
prolata lucerna et adrepta novacula sexum audacia
mutatur. sed cum primum luminis oblatione tori   2
5   secreta claruerunt, videt omnium ferarum mitissimam
dulcissimamque bestiam, ipsum illum Cupidinem
formonsum deum formonse cubantem, cuius aspectu
lucernae quoque lumen hilaratum increbruit et acuminis
sacrilegi novacula praenitebat. at vero Psyche tanto   3
10   aspectu deterrita et impos animi marcido pallore defecta
tremensque desedit in imos poplites et ferrum quaerit
abscondere, sed in suo pectore; quod profecto fecisset,   4
nisi ferrum, timore tanti flagitii, manibus temerariis
delapsum evolasset. iamque lassa, salute defecta, dum

15 saepius divini vultus intuetur pulchritudinem, recreatur

animi. videt capitis aurei genialem caesariem ambrosia   5

temulentam, cervices lacteas genasque purpureas

pererrantes crinium globos decoriter impeditos, alios

antependulos, alios retropendulos, quorum splendore

20 nimio fulgurante iam et ipsum lumen lucernae vacillabat;

per umeros volatilis dei pinnae roscidae micanti flore   6

candicant et quamvis alis quiescentibus extimae

plumulae tenellae ac delicatae tremule resultantes

inquieta lasciviunt; ceterum corpus glabellum atque   7

25 luculentum et quale peperisse Venerem non paeniteret.

ante lectuli pedes iacebat arcus et pharetra et sagittae,

magni dei propitia tela.

5.23 quae dum insatiabili animo Psyche, satis et curiosa,   1

rimatur atque pertrectat et mariti sui miratur arma,

30 depromit unam de pharetra sagittam et punctu pollicis   2

extremam aciem periclitabunda trementis etiam nunc

articuli nisu fortiore pupugit altius, ut per summam

cutem roraverint parvulae sanguinis rosei guttae. sic   3

ignara Psyche sponte in Amoris incidit amorem. tunc

35 magis magisque cupidine fraglans Cupidinis prona in

eum efflictim inhians patulis ac petulantibus saviis

festinanter ingestis de somni mensura metuebat. sed   4

dum bono tanto percita saucia mente fluctuat, lucerna

illa, sive perfidia pessima sive invidia noxia sive quod

40 tale corpus contingere et quasi basiare et ipsa gestiebat,

evomuit de summa luminis sui stillam ferventis olei

super umerum dei dexterum. hem audax et temeraria   5

lucerna et amoris vile ministerium, ipsum ignis totius

deum aduris, cum te scilicet amator aliquis, ut diutius

45 cupitis etiam nocte potiretur, primus invenerit. sic   6

inustus exiluit deus visaque detectae fidei colluvie

prorsus ex osculis et manibus infelicissimae coniugis

tacitus avolavit.

Book 6
6.20–21

6.20 Sic turris illa prospicua vaticinationis munus   1
explicuit. nec morata Psyche pergit Taenarum,
sumptisque rite stipibus illis et offulis, infernum decurrit
meatum, transitoque per silentium asinario debili, et   2
5   amnica stipe vectori data, neglecto supernatantis mortui
desiderio, et spretis textricum subdolis precibus, et
offulae cibo sopita canis horrenda rabie, domum
Proserpinae penetrat. nec offerentis hospitae sedile   3
delicatum vel cibum beatum amplexa, sed ante pedes
10 eius residens humilis, cibario pane contenta, Veneriam
pertulit legationem. statimque secreto repletam   4
conclusamque pyxidem suscipit et offulae sequentis
fraude caninis latratibus obseratis, residuaque navitae
reddita stipe, longe vegetior ab inferis recurrit. et repetita   5
15 atque adorata candida ista luce, quanquam festinans
obsequium terminare, mentem capitur temeraria
curiositate et: 'ecce' inquit 'inepta ego divinae   6
formonsitatis gerula, quae nec tantillum quidem indidem
mihi delibo vel sic illi amatori meo formonso placitura,'
20 **6.21** et cum dicto reserat pyxidem. nec quicquam ibi   1
rerum nec formonsitas ulla, sed infernus somnus
ac vere Stygius, qui statim coperculo revelatus invadit
eam crassaque soporis nebula cunctis eius membris
perfunditur et in ipso vestigio ipsaque semita conlapsam

25 possidet. et iacebat immobilis et nihil aliud quam   2

dormiens cadaver. sed Cupido iam cicatrice solida

revalescens nec diutinam suae Psyches absentiam

tolerans per altissimam cubiculi quo cohibebatur elapsus

fenestram refectisque pinnis aliquanta quiete longe   3

30 velocius provolans Psychen accurrit suam detersoque

somno curiose et rursum in pristinam pyxidis sedem

recondito Psychen innoxio punctulo sagittae suae suscitat

et: 'ecce' inquit 'rursum perieras, misella, simili   4

curiositate. sed interim quidem tu provinciam quae tibi

35 matris meae praecepto mandata est exsequere naviter,

cetera egomet videro.' his dictis amator levis in pinnas se

dedit, Psyche vero confestim Veneri munus reportat

Proserpinae.

6.23.5–6.24.4

6.23 . . . ilico per Mercurium arripi Psychen et in caelum   5

perduci iubet. porrecto ambrosiae poculo: 'sume,' inquit

'Psyche, et immortalis esto, nec umquam digredietur a

tuo nexu Cupido sed istae vobis erunt perpetuae nuptiae.'

5 **6.24** Nec mora, cum cena nuptialis affluens exhibetur.   1

accumbebat summum torum maritus, Psychen gremio

suo complexus. sic et cum sua Iunone Iuppiter ac deinde

per ordinem toti dei. tunc poculum nectaris, quod vinum   2

deorum est, Iovi quidem suus pocillator ille rusticus puer,

10 ceteris vero Liber ministrabat, Vulcanus cenam coquebat;

Horae rosis et ceteris floribus purpurabant omnia,   3

Gratiae spargebant balsama, Musae quoque canora

personabant. Apollo cantavit ad citharam, Venus suavi

musicae superingressa formonsa saltavit, scaena sibi sic

15   concinnata, ut Musae quidem chorum canerent, tibias

inflaret Saturus, et Paniscus ad fistulam diceret. sic rite   4

Psyche convenit in manum Cupidinis et nascitur illis

maturo partu filia, quam Voluptatem nominamus."

Book 9
9.12.2–9.13.5

9.12 at ego, quanquam eximie fatigatus et refectione   2
virium vehementer indiguus et prorsus fame perditus,
tamen familiari curiositate attonitus et satis anxius,
postposito cibo, qui copiosus aderat, inoptabilis officinae
5 disciplinam cum delectatione quadam arbitrabar. dii   3
boni, quales illic homunculi vibicibus lividis totam cutem
depicti dorsumque plagosum scissili centunculo magis
inumbrati quam obtecti, nonnulli exiguo tegili tantum
modo pubem iniecti, cuncti tamen sic tunicati ut essent   4
10 per pannulos manifesti, frontes litterati et capillum
semirasi et pedes anulati, tum lurore deformes et fumosis
tenebris vaporosae caliginis palpebras adesi atque adeo
male luminati et in modum pugilum, qui pulvisculo
perspersi dimicant, farinulenta cinere sordide candidati.
15 **9.13** iam de meo iumentario contubernio quid vel ad   1
quem modum memorem? quales illi muli senes vel
cantherii debiles. circa praesepium capita demersi   2
contruncabant moles palearum, cervices cariosa
vulnerum putredine follicantes, nares languidas adsiduo
20 pulsu tussedinis hiulci, pectora copulae sparteae tritura
continua exulcerati, costas perpetua castigatione ossium
tenus renudati, ungulas multivia circumcursione in
enorme vestigium porrecti totumque corium veterno
atque scabiosa macie exasperati. talis familiae funestum   3
25 mihi etiam metuens exemplum veterisque Lucii fortunam
recordatus et ad ultimam salutis metam detrusus

summisso capite maerebam. nec ullum uspiam cruciabilis
vitae solacium aderat, nisi quod ingenita mihi curiositate
recreabar, dum praesentiam meam parvi facientes, libere,
30   quae volunt, omnes et agunt et loquuntur. nec inmerito   4
priscae poeticae divinus auctor apud Graios summae
prudentiae virum monstrare cupiens multarum civitatium
obitu et variorum populorum cognitu summas adeptum
virtutes cecinit. nam et ipse gratas gratias asino meo   5
35   memini, quod me suo celatum tegmine variisque fortunis
exercitatum, etsi minus prudentem, multiscium reddidit.

Book 10
10.16.7–10.17.6

10.16 Quod dictum dominus secutus: "non adeo"   7
respondit "absurde iocatus es, furcifer; valde enim fieri
potest, ut contubernalis noster poculum quoque mulsi
libenter adpetat." et "heus," ait "puer, lautum diligenter   8
5   ecce illum aureum cantharum mulso contempera et offer
parasito meo; simul, quod ei praebiberim, commoneto."
ingens exin oborta est epulonum exspectatio. Nec ulla   9
tamen ego ratione conterritus, otiose ac satis genialiter
contorta in modum linguae postrema labia grandissimum
10 illum calicem uno haustu perduxi. et clamor exurgit
consona voce cunctorum salute me prosequentium.
10.17 magno denique delibutus gaudio dominus, vocatis   1
servis suis emptoribus meis, iubet quadruplum restitui
pretium, meque cuidam acceptissimo liberto suo et satis
15 peculiato, magnam praefatus diligentiam, tradidit. qui   2
me satis humane satisque comiter nutriebat et, quo se
patrono commendatiorem faceret, studiosissime
voluptates eius per meas argutias instruebat. et primum   3
me quidem mensam accumbere suffixo cubito, dein
20 adluctari et etiam saltare sublatis primoribus pedibus
perdocuit, quodque esset adprime mirabile, verbis nutum   4
commodare, ut quod nollem relato, quod vellem deiecto
capite monstrarem, sitiensque pocillatore respecto, ciliis
alterna conivens, bibere flagitarem. atque haec omnia   5
25 perfacile oboediebam, quae nullo etiam monstrante
scilicet facerem. sed verebar ne, si forte sine magistro

humano ritu ederem pleraque, rati scaevum praesagium

portendere, velut monstrum ostentumque me obtruncatum

vulturiis opimum pabulum redderent. iamque rumor   6

30 publice crebruerat, quo conspectum atque famigerabilem

meis miris artibus effeceram dominum: hic est, qui

sodalem convivamque possidet asinum luctantem,

asinum saltantem, asinum voces humanas intellegentem,

sensum nutibus exprimentem.

Book 11
11.1–2

11.1 Circa primam ferme noctis vigiliam experrectus   1
pavore subito, video praemicantis lunae candore nimio
completum orbem commodum marinis emergentem
fluctibus; nanctusque opacae noctis silentiosa secreta,
5   certus etiam summatem deam praecipua maiestate   2
pollere resque prorsus humanas ipsius regi providentia,
nec tantum pecuina et ferina, verum inanima etiam
divino eius luminis numinisque nutu vegetari, ipsa etiam
corpora terra caelo marique nunc incrementis
10   consequenter augeri, nunc detrimentis obsequenter
imminui, fato scilicet iam meis tot tantisque cladibus   3
satiato et spem salutis, licet tardam, subministrante,
augustum specimen deae praesentis statui deprecari;
confestimque discussa pigra quiete alacer exsurgo meque   4
15   protinus purificandi studio marino lavacro trado
septiesque summerso fluctibus capite, quod eum
numerum praecipue religionibus aptissimum divinus ille
Pythagoras prodidit, laetus et alacer deam praepotentem
lacrimoso vultu sic adprecabar:
20   **11.2** "Regina caeli, — sive tu Ceres alma frugum parens   1
originalis, quae, repertu laetata filiae, vetustae glandis
ferino remoto pabulo, miti commonstrato cibo nunc
Eleusiniam glebam percolis, seu tu caelestis Venus, quae
primis rerum exordiis sexuum diversitatem generato
25   Amore sociasti et aeterna subole humano genere
propagato nunc circumfluo Paphi sacrario coleris, seu   2

Phoebi soror, quae partu fetarum medelis lenientibus

recreato populos tantos educasti praeclarisque nunc

veneraris delubris Ephesi, seu nocturnis ululatibus

30   horrenda Proserpina triformi facie larvales impetus

comprimens terraeque claustra cohibens lucos diversos

inerrans vario cultu propitiaris, — ista luce feminea   3

conlustrans cuncta moenia et udis ignibus nutriens laeta

semina et solis ambagibus dispensans incerta lumina,

35   quoquo nomine, quoquo ritu, quaqua facie te fas est

invocare: tu meis iam nunc extremis aerumnis subsiste,   4

tu fortunam conlapsam adfirma, tu saevis exanclatis

casibus pausam pacemque tribue; sit satis laborum, sit

satis periculorum. depelle quadripedis diram faciem,

40   redde me conspectui meorum, redde me meo Lucio, ac

si quod offensum numen inexorabili me saevitia premit,

mori saltem liceat, si non licet vivere."

11.5.1 and 11.5.3–4

11.5 "En adsum tuis commota, Luci, precibus, rerum   1

naturae parens, elementorum omnium domina,

saeculorum progenies initialis, summa numinum,

regina manium, prima caelitum, deorum dearumque

5   facies uniformis, quae caeli luminosa culmina, maris

salubria flamina, inferum deplorata silentia nutibus meis

dispenso: cuius numen unicum multiformi specie, ritu

vario, nomine multiiugo totus veneratur orbis.

. . . Aethiopes utrique priscaque doctrina pollentes   3

10   Aegyptii caerimoniis me propriis percolentes appellant

vero nomine reginam Isidem. adsum tuos miserata   4
casus, adsum favens et propitia. mitte iam fletus et
lamentationes omitte, depelle maerorem; iam tibi
providentia mea inlucescit dies salutaris."

11.13

11.13 at sacerdos, ut reabse cognoscere potui, nocturni   1
commonefactus oraculi miratusque congruentiam
mandati muneris, confestim restitit et, ultro porrecta
dextera, ob os ipsum meum coronam exhibuit. tunc ego   2
5   trepidans, adsiduo pulsu micanti corde, coronam, quae
rosis amoenis intexta fulgurabat, avido ore susceptam
cupidus promissi devoravi. nec me fefellit caeleste   3
promissum: protinus mihi delabitur deformis et ferina
facies. ac primo quidem squalens pilus defluit, ac dehinc   4
10 cutis crassa tenuatur, venter obesus residet, pedum
plantae per ungulas in digitos exeunt, manus non iam
pedes sunt, sed in erecta porriguntur officia, cervix   5
procera cohibetur, os et caput rutundatur, aures enormes
repetunt pristinam parvitatem, dentes saxei redeunt ad
15 humanam minutiem, et, quae me potissimum cruciabat
ante, cauda nusquam! populi mirantur, religiosi   6
venerantur tam evidentem maximi numinis potentiam
et consimilem nocturnis imaginibus magnificentiam et
facilitatem reformationis, claraque et consona voce,
20 caelo manus adtendentes, testantur tam inlustre deae
beneficium.

11.15.1–3

11.15 "Multis et variis exanclatis laboribus magnisque 1
Fortunae tempestatibus et maximis actus procellis ad
portum Quietis et aram Misericordiae tandem, Luci,
venisti. nec tibi natales ac ne dignitas quidem, vel ipsa,
5   qua flores, usquam doctrina profuit, sed lubrico virentis
aetatulae ad serviles delapsus voluptates curiositatis
inprosperae sinistrum praemium reportasti. sed 2
utcumque Fortunae caecitas, dum te pessimis periculis
discruciat, ad religiosam istam beatitudinem inprovida
10   produxit malitia. eat nunc et summo furore saeviat et
crudelitati suae materiem quaerat aliam; nam in eos,
quorum sibi vitas in servitium deae nostrae maiestas
vindicavit, non habet locum casus infestus. quid latrones, 3
quid ferae, quid servitium, quid asperrimorum itinerum
15   ambages reciprocae, quid metus mortis cotidianae
nefariae Fortunae profuit? In tutelam iam receptus es
Fortunae, sed videntis, quae suae lucis splendore ceteros
etiam deos illuminat . . ."

11.27.9

11.27 nam sibi visus est quiete proxima, dum magno deo 9
coronas exaptat, . . . et de eius ore, quo singulorum fata
dictat, audisse mitti sibi Madaurensem, sed admodum
pauperem, cui statim sua sacra deberet ministrare; nam
5   et illi studiorum gloriam et ipsi grande compendium sua
comparari providentia.

11.30.3–5

11.30 denique post dies admodum pauculos deus deum   3
magnorum potior et maiorum summus et summorum
maximus et maximorum regnator Osiris non in alienam
quampiam personam reformatus, sed coram suo illo
5 venerando me dignatus adfamine per quietem recipere
visus est: quam nunc, incunctanter gloriosa in foro   4
redderem patrocinia, nec extimescerem malevolorum
disseminationes, quas studiorum meorum laboriosa
doctrina ibidem exciverat. ac ne sacris suis gregi cetero
10 permixtus deservirem, in collegium me pastophorum
suorum immo inter ipsos decurionum quinquennales
adlegit. rursus denique quaqua raso capillo, collegii   5
vetustissimi et sub illis Sullae temporibus conditi munia,
non obumbrato vel obtecto calvitio, sed quoquoversus
15 obvio, gaudens obibam.

Commentary

Abbreviations of references used in the commentary:

> A&G: *Allen and Greenough's New Latin Grammar,*
> Boston 1903.
> Bradley's Arnold: *Bradley's Arnold, Latin Prose*
> *Composition,* New York 1938.
> GCA: *Groningen Commentaries on Apuleius,* various
> editors
> OLD: *Oxford Latin Dictionary.* Oxford 1982.

∾ *METAMORPHOSES*

Book 1

1.1.1–1.2.1 The prologue and a bit more

1.1   Much has been written on this one complicated section of the
Metamorphoses. In fact, a whole book was published on this
section alone (Kahane and Laird 2001). The prologue introduc-
es us to the work and particularly to its narrator—or is it the
author, or does a conversation take place between the author
and an interlocutor? It has also been suggested that the speaker
of the prologue is the book itself, a trope seen, for example, at
the beginning of Ovid's *Amores.* Whoever he is, he promises
us delightful tales and pleasure, hints at metamorphoses and
Egyptian material, and introduces himself as a Greek in origin
and someone whose native language was not Latin.

1.1.1   **At** an unusual way to begin a work, though *Aeneid* 4 begins
"At regina . . . " It seems to imply that the speaker was in the
midst of a conversation already.

ego tibi Note the very personal way the work introduces it-self—I, to you.

sermone isto Milesio "in that Milesian style." Critics see here a reference to the so-called "Milesian Tale," perhaps characterized by immorality and sex, but little understood. Aristides of Miletus was the originator of the genre ca. 100 BCE, and Sisenna several decades later adapted his style or his tales into Latin. Miletus (in Asia Minor) is also mentioned at 4.32 in the introduction to the "Tale of Cupid and Psyche," which, however, is not scandalous. Tilg (2007) has recently revived discussion of the Milesian Tale, looking at fragments of Sisenna's other works and finding them stylistically rebellious and akin to Apuleius. It may be style more than content to which the speaker here refers.

fabulas The speaker promises *fabulae*, that is, humble "tales" rather than grand epic or stories of gods and heroes.

conseram The verb could be fut. tense, but since *permulceam* has to be subjunctive, *conseram* probably is as well; both are easily understood as jussive subjunctives.

sermone, aures, susurro Note the emphasis on hearing oral tales, which is complicated by references to writing and seeing in the next clause.

papyrum Aegyptiam . . . Nilotici calami *papyrus* is feminine, like many plants of the second declension. Egypt was the origin of much papyrus in the ancient world and was also known as the birthplace of writing. Yet, for someone who knows the ending, this epithet also hints at the resolution of the work and the intervention of the Egyptian goddess, Isis.

1.1.2 **figuras fortunasque . . . ut mireris** "so that you may wonder at the forms and fortunes . . ." The verb and its governing *ut* are postponed to the end. The narrator mentions plural meta-morphoses, so the subject is not just Lucius, but others as well. Keulen (2007) punctuates as *ut mireris exordior*: "I begin so that you may wonder."

mutuo nexu "with reciprocal intertwining." This seems to mean that the transformations and re-transformations are deeply interconnected. *Nexus* evokes the twisting and binding that is integral to magic spells (cf. 3.18).

1.1.3 **exordior. quis ille?** Some translate *quis ille* as "who am I?" but the use of *ille* within a first person narration is confusing. Is the speaker referring to himself with the word *ille*; does it imply *ille ego* for example, or is there another speaker? Scholars have suggested that, as in Plautine prologues, a dialogue takes place. Someone else, perhaps even the reader, asks "who is that?" after which the original speaker comes back in and identifies himself.

paucis sc. *verbis*

Hymettos Attica et Isthmos Ephyrea et Taenaros Spartiaca Essentially the speaker says, "my origins are Athens, Corinth, and Sparta," naming the three most important cities in Greece, but he does so in a rather baroque manner. He makes the names of the cities adjs. and attaches them to familiar landmarks. He also changes the gender of all three landmarks; normally, Hymettos, Isthmos, and Taenaros would be masculine. Hymettos (Greek nom.) is a mountain near Athens famous for its honey. Ephyre was the ancient name for Corinth, a city known for its isthmus (now a canal); Taenaros was a promontory near Sparta.

glebae felices aeternum libris felicioribus conditae "fertile lands preserved forever in even more fertile books." *aeternum* is adverbial. *glebae* are literally clumps of soil, so there is strong agricultural imagery here, but with a pitch for the endurance of literature.

mea vetus prosapia est *prosapia* is an archaic word, lending the statement dignity appropriate to the speaker's ancestry. The speaker here clearly gives a Greek ancestry, leading us to believe that he is Lucius the Greek narrator rather than Apuleius the African author, but the ancestry in question is very much a literary one, considering that no real Greek would claim to be simultaneously Athenian, Corinthian, and Spartan. Thus, the identity of the speaker is left open.

1.1.4 **linguam Attidem primis pueritiae stipendiis merui** The speaker uses the imagery of the military campaign to describe his acquisition of Greek. "I earned (*merui*) the Attic tongue in the first campaigns of my youth." The Attic tongue may refer specifically to the Attic dialect of Greek, or may just mean "Greek" more generally. If the narrator is strictly Lucius, a Greek, and not the author to any degree, it would be surprising for him to refer to his *learning* Greek. Perhaps, then, the reference would be to learning *Attic* Greek in particular, as Lucius later reveals that he is from Corinth. On the other hand, if the narrator is partly Apuleius, a North African, then both the reference to learning Greek and to learning Latin with difficulty are more apt.

advena studiorum Quiritium "a newcomer to Roman studies." This designation could apply well to either Lucius the Greek or Apuleius the North African.

aerumnabili labore Any Latin student should sympathize with this statement!

aggressus excolui perhaps continuing the military imagery: "I attacked and cultivated"

1.1.5 **siquid** i.e., *si quid*, where (*ali*) *quid* is adverbial: "if at all"

exotici ac forensis sermonis The speaker either claims to write "foreign and forensic" Latin or "foreign and outsider" Latin. *Exoticus* means "foreign," which is a somewhat surprising designation for Latin, the dominant imperial language of the age and obviously the language in which the work is written. Calling it "exoticus" indicates that the speaker comes from somewhere else and de-centers Latin and Rome. *Forensis* normally means "of the Forum," but it has been suggested that here it derives from *foris* (outside Rome, abroad), a synonym of *exoticus*.

rudis locutor There may be a pun here on *rudere*: to bray (like a donkey). The speaker implies, in any case, that his Latin is rough, unpolished and non-native. Of course, Apuleius' language is anything but crude and halting, though different from Classical Latin (see Introduction). In part, this whole apology is a *captatio benevolentiae*, a pose designed to gain our goodwill, but also sets up the identity of the speaker as a foreigner. If we accept the legitimacy of the pun on *rudere*, then speaking the rough Latin of a foreigner is equated with being a donkey and the book may be read as a metaphorical journey of the foreign immigrant to Rome. Tilg (2007) doubts the legitimacy of the pun and interprets "rudis" to mean "rough" quite literally; the Latin we will read is not the Latin of Cicero, but deliberately the Latin of old wives' tales.

1.1.6   **vocis immutatio** Given the preceding apologies for foreign Latin, the *immutatio* is likely to refer to a change from normative to foreign Latin. Tilg (2007) points out that *immutatio* is a rhetorical term that refers to deviation (either by error or deliberately) from standard Latin and thus argues that once again Apuleius is announcing something about his anomalous style (not, however, in Tilg's view, to be attributed to foreignness, but simple choice and appropriateness to the subject-matter). The phrase has previously been read as a reference to the change from Greek to Latin (*fabulam Graecanicam*).

desultoriae scientiae stilo "the mode of composition that resembles the skill of circus-jumpers." A *desultor* is an acrobat in the circus who jumps from one horse to another. This could be used as an image for the change from Greek to Latin, but could more generally refer to the book's construction in which the narrator jumps rapidly from one topic to the next, via the embedded tales. So, perhaps, the unusual language corresponds to the unusual mode of composition; style is matched to content.

laetaberis The focus on pleasure should not, of course, blind us to the more serious subjects and themes of the book.

1.2   Lucius sets out on a journey on business

Here, the speaker is clearly Lucius, as he begins to narrate the story of his travels.

1.2.1   **Thessaliam** a region of Greece particularly associated with witchcraft

fundamenta . . . prodita "the foundations . . . established by"

originis maternae Given that this is a fictional ancestry, it is striking that Lucius chooses to make Plutarch his relative on his *mother's* side in the highly patriarchal Graeco-Roman world. The lineage is mentioned again when Lucius meets his maternal aunt at 2.2–3. The work is full of reversals of gender roles and hierarchies.

Plutarcho illo inclito the famous Plutarch of Chaeronea (not actually of Thessaly), Greek author (ca. 45–125 CE) most famous now for his *Parallel Lives,* a philosopher and prolific polymath. He wrote a treatise *On Isis and Osiris,* which makes him an appropriate fictional ancestor for Lucius, as well as several dialogues and treatises challenging accepted views on the rationality of animals—again an appropriate connection to this work.

Sexto philosopho nepote eius Sextus of Chaeronea, philosopher whose work is now lost, nephew of Plutarch (though *nepos* means "grandson" or "descendant" in Classical Latin), taught Marcus Aurelius. It has been suggested that he was one of Apuleius' teachers in Athens.

eam Thessaliam repeated object, creating the impression of a spoken style

Book 2

2.1.1–2.2.1 Thessaly and magic

In Book 1, Lucius encountered several other travelers who told stories along the way to ease the journey—stories about witchcraft and robbers. He has a letter of introduction to a prominent citizen, Milo, at whose house he stays. Arrived in Thessaly, Lucius is eager to encounter magic, and his hopes and desires make him hyper-alert, but also distort his perception of everything around him.

2.1.1   Long sentence. Sort out its components. Note the many pples. and adjs. agreeing with the subject (I, Lucius): *emersus, anxius, cupidus, reputans, suspensus.*

Ut primum . . . fecit The elaborate phrases describe a sunrise; several books of the *Metamorphoses* start this way.

sol novus poetic; transferred epithet (hypallage); obviously the day and not the sun is new.

emersus The pf. pple. is here act., as often (OLD *emergo* 1 b).

et somno simul emersus et lectulo zeugma, which conveys Lucius' impatience: he is out of bed as soon as he wakes up.

nimis cupidus *nimis* here means "very, exceedingly," an archaizing usage, but a reader familiar with the later developments of the novel will also hear the more standard meaning: "too." Lucius is perhaps too curious about magic.

cupidus cognoscendi "desirous of knowing"; *cognoscendi* is gen. of the gerund

quae rara miraque sunt n. pl. object of *cognoscendi,* "things which . . ."

2.1.2   **qua . . . celebrentur** subjunctive in a subordinate clause within indirect discourse (A&G 580)

totius orbis consono ore "by the voice of the whole world singing in unison"

Aristomenis In Book 1, Lucius met a traveler named Aristomenes, who told a tale about witches.

de situ civitatis huius a wordy way of saying "in this city," i.e., Hypata, in Thessaly

curiose (adv.) here means both "with great care" and "curiously."

2.1.3   **nec fuit . . . quod aspiciens id esse crederem quod esset** "there was nothing which, as I looked at it, I believed to be what it was"

prorsus a favorite Apuleian word: "absolutely, totally," here probably to be construed with *omnia*

translata supply *esse crederem*

2.1.4   **ut . . . crederem** result clause, with *crederem* introducing an indirect statement involving a series of infinitives: *duratos, plumatas, foliatas, fluxos <esse>*. Subjunctives in subordinate clauses within indirect discourse (*offenderem, audirem, ambirent*), as with *qua . . . celebrentur* above.

indidem "from the same stuff," i.e., also made from transformed humans

2.1.5   **id genus pecua** "cattle of this sort," adverbial acc.

iubaris orbe i.e., the sun; an archaic and poetic usage

2.2.1   **attonitus, stupidus** Both words convey Lucius' state of shock. *Stupidus* is presented as the stronger emotion; *immo vero,* "more accurately," expresses a slight correction of *attonitus.*

nullo initio, vel omnino vestigio reperto abl. absolute. Lucius is not finding the magic he desires to find.

2.6–7 Fotis cooking

In 2.2–5, Lucius' aunt Byrrhaena, who has mysteriously encountered him in the forum, warns Lucius that his host Milo's wife, Pamphile, is a witch and that Lucius must keep away from her. Naturally, the warning has the opposite of the intended effect; Lucius is on the way to gaining access to the magic he so desires. However, he vows to keep away from his host's wife and instead pursue his goal by seducing the slave, Fotis (Photis).

2.6.1 **curiosus alioquin** *alioquin* expresses the idea that Lucius had already, in any case, been curious, but his curiosity is heightened by his aunt's warnings.

ut primum, "as soon as"

tantum . . . ut result clause

Pamphiles Greek gen.; objective gen., i.e., caution *against* Pamphile

2.6.2 **barathrum** (from the Greek *barathron*) a pit, either man-made or referring to the Underworld, Tartarus. Lucius seems to mean, with a degree of self-irony, that he is eager to throw himself into the dark unknown pit of the forbidden supernatural.

memet intensive form of *me*, from *egomet*

2.6.3 **salve** Clearly Lucius is saying "good-bye" here, not hello, a rarer but well-attested meaning.

2.6.4 **tecum esto** "get control of yourself"; Lucius here addresses himself (like Catullus in, e.g., poem 52).

2.6.5 **voto diutino** "according to the desire you have held for so long"

2.6.6 **aufer, etc.** Note the string of imperatives; Lucius is still exhorting himself.

religiosus Latin uses an adj. where English would use an adv.: "reverently."

verum enimvero The combination is not only intensive, but involves a transition to another topic: but (*verum*) truly (*enimvero*).

Fotis The orthography in the manuscripts varies; sometimes the slave-girl is called Fotis and sometimes Photis. This book retains those variations in the Latin text, but will refer to her in the notes consistently as "Fotis" because this is the most commonly used variant in current criticism.

petatur jussive subjunctive

2.6.7 **osculato tuo capite** abl. absolute

quam invita discederet vultu prodidit "she betrayed with her face how (*quam*) unwillingly she was leaving." The whole scene reveals rather forward behavior on Fotis' part.

quod bonum felix faustumque . . . licet non salutare The first part of the phrase echoes a religious formula spoken to ratify actions of the senate, but Lucius follows this up with a recognition that his actions could end badly. *Licet* is concessive.

2.7.1 **pedibus in sententiam vado** Lucius "votes with his feet," a figure taken from the practice in the Roman senate where senators showed support for a motion by walking to a particular side.

2.7.2 **viscum fartim concisum et pulpam frustatim consectam** "innards chopped into pieces and flesh minced fine." The exact meaning is in doubt, but Fotis is preparing a meal entirely of meat, not uncommon in antiquity.

†**ambacu pascuae**† textual crux, i.e., the transmitted manuscript makes no sense and cannot be convincingly emended. Supply your food of choice.

perquam sapidissimum *perquam* ("extremely") is added to a superl. for a super-superlative effect, first attested here.

2.7.3 **mundule amicta** Notice the abundance of diminutives here, some of them (*mundule, altiuscule, succinctula*) apparently coined by Apuleius, expressing erotic interest rather than petiteness.

russea fasceola praenitente . . . succinctula "prettily girded up with a bright red breastband"; *russea fasceola* is abl., *succinctula* is nom. Women fastened their tunics with a strip of cloth tied beneath their breasts.

succinctula *succinctus* plus a diminutive ending

altiuscule *altius* (compar. adv.) with a diminutive adverbial ending

rotabat She was turning the pot in circles. Although we imagine a spoon, she apparently is simply rotating the pot itself.

in orbis flexibus crebra succutiens "shaking it frequently in her circular movements" (*crebra* is adverbial acc.)

decenter "charmingly" rather than "decently," though humorously alluding to the standard meaning

2.7.4   **isto aspectu defixus obstupui . . . steterunt** These lines rather ironically recall *Aeneid* 2.774: "*obstipui steteruntque comae*" (Aeneas seeing Creusa's ghost) as well *Aen.* 1.613: "*obstipuit primo aspectu Sidonia Dido*" (Dido's first sight of Aeneas). Apuleius is fond of importing epic language into his novel in contexts which contrast sharply with the original yet involve a clever overlap of content—in this case, the encounter of the central character with women with whom he has some erotic or love interest. The effect is comic and questions the loftiness of epic and its themes, but also introduces epic language into this lower genre, playing with generic distinctions. See further Finkelpearl 1998.

membra quae iacebant ante erotic sense

2.7.6   **certo certius** "surer than sure" i.e., absolutely

2.7.7   **quam procul,** "as far as possible," an extension of the use of *quam* to intensify superls.

si te . . . meus igniculus afflaverit, ureris intime nec ullus extinguet fut. more vivid condition with fut. pf. tense in the protasis, futs. in the apodosis

suave quatere *suave* is a n. adj. used adverbially.

Book 3

In the intervening sections, Lucius and Fotis have become lovers
(obviously). Lucius attends a dinner at his aunt Byrrhaena's house
at which he hears more stories of witchcraft. Fotis has warned him
that he should not return too late at night because bands of dan-
gerous youth are terrorizing the neighborhood. When he nears Mi-
lo's house, Lucius sees three enormous figures trying with all their
strength to break down the door, and he draws his sword and slaugh-
ters them all. This act of Lucius' sets the scene for the year's celebra-
tion of the Festival of Laughter in Hypata. See further discussion at
the end of this selection.

3.1.1–3.2.5 Lucius is apprehended

3.1.1 **Commodum . . . et** "at this very moment . . . and I"; i.e., "it was
just at this moment when . . . " Note another sunrise, this time,
something of a parody of the Homeric "rosy-fingered dawn,"
which appears about twenty times in the *Odyssey*; e.g., 2.1.

punicantibus phaleris "Aurora with her reddening trap-
pings," abl. of description, though really the horses are wear-
ing the trappings, not Aurora. *Punicans* is an Apuleian in-
vention; *phalerae* are ornamental trappings placed on the
forehead and breast of horses.

me securae quieti revulsum "me, torn from an untroubled
sleep," *quieti* is dat. after *revello*; object of (*nox*) *reddidit*.

3.1.2 **vesperni recordatione facinoris** "at the recollection of the
evening's deed" i.e., the killing of the "robbers"

complicitis . . . conexis an elaborate and very Apuleian way of
saying that Lucius was sitting with his knees drawn up to his
chest and his arms wrapped around them

palmulis in alternas digitorum vicissitudines . . . conexis
"with my hands entwined in(to) alternating interchanges of
my fingers" i.e., with my hands clasped

sententiam here obviously meaning "the (judicial) sentenc-
ing." Turpin (2002) points out that Lucius is thinking of the

various stages of the trial: first being brought to the forum, then undergoing the trial (*iudicia*), then the sentencing, and finally the executioner (*carnifex*).

imaginabundus The word appears only here (*hapax legomenon*): "imagining."

3.1.3 **tam mitis ... qui ... poterit** Lucius uses a construction more casual than a result clause. In Classical Latin, one might expect the standard rel. result clause with the subjunctive, *tam mitis qui* (= *ut*) *possit*, but Lucius uses the fut. indicative (*poterit*), perhaps reflecting everyday spoken usage.

3.1.4 **hanc illam peregrinationem** "so this is the glorious voyage . . ."

Chaldaeus Diophanes At 2.12, Lucius tells Milo that he met a fortune-teller of this name who foretold that he (Lucius) would win glory and become an incredible tale and a book.

3.1.5 **quati, perstrepi** historical infinitives, here used to express the suddenness of the banging at the door

3.2.1 **nec mora cum** "there was no delay when . . ." i.e., "at once"

magistratibus eorumque ministris et turbae miscellaneae cuncta completa sc. *sunt*; "Everything was filled with magistrates and their assistants and a mixed crowd." If we accept this reading, then *completa* takes first the abl. and then the gen. This kind of mixed construction is rare but not unparalleled in Apuleius and also in Sallust.

immissa manu abl. absolute, "laying his hands on me," i.e., arresting me. *manum inicere* (and in Apuleius *manum immittere*) is the legal term for seizing someone on whom one has a legal claim.

3.2.3 **capite ... deiecto** abl. absolute

lictores Note the distinctly Roman civic apparatus although the story takes place in Greece. The lictors accompany the magistrates both as a mark of honor and in order to do the heavy work, somewhat like police. In Book 1, they were the ones ordered to trample the overly priced fish, and see below.

obliquato aspectu "out of the corner of my eye"

rem admirationis maximae i.e., *rem maxime admirabilem*

3.2.4 **prorsum** intensifying *nemo*, "absolutely nobody"

In the brief intervening sections, Lucius is led through the streets into the forum and in front of the tribunal, a platform for judicial proceedings, but the crowd demands that the trial take place in the theater because of overcrowding.

3.2.7–9 A crowd gathers

3.2.7 **passim populus . . . complevit** Note the alliteration of *p* and *c*, extreme alliteration being one of the features of Apuleius' ornate style.

3.2.8 **lacunaria** These are properly ceiling panels, but they must contain some gaps so that the viewers can see and be *semiconspicui*.

3.2.9 **velut quandam victimam** i.e., like a sacrificial victim, a cow or pig, but also indicating perhaps that Lucius is a kind of scapegoat

publica ministeria n.pl. for m. (*ministri*), referring to the attendants who were earlier mentioned as serving the magistrates

orchestrae mediae "they place me in the middle of the orchestra"; probably dat., as Apuleius also constructs *sisto* with a dat. at 4.34. The *proscaenium* of a Roman theater is the stage. In front of the stage, nearer to the spectators is the *orchestra* where there was sometimes dancing and which sometimes included seating for distinguished guests. The "trial" takes place conspicuously in the theater rather than a court, emphasizing its character as entertainment—as we eventually learn.

3.8.1–4 The widows plead for vengeance

In the intervening sections, the prosecutor lays out the case: that Lucius viciously killed three young men and fled. Lucius defends his actions, admitting the killing, but saying that the men were breaking down Milo's door and trying to enter. He invents a pitched battle between himself and the robbers and pleads for mercy on the grounds that he was doing his duty by his host, Milo. The whole scene is a parody of the courtroom, and uses many motifs of standard literary parodies of the court, including the following pity-inducing speech by a distraught woman.

3.8.1   **anus alia** "another woman, an old one," or "an old woman as well," rather than "another old woman." The first woman is evidently young since she holds a baby. This is a common use of *alius*; OLD *alius* 5.

    ramos oleagineos While olive branches normally symbolize peace, they are also connected with supplication.

3.8.2   **contexta fuerant** for *contexta erant*; this anomalous form of the plpf. appears elsewhere in Apuleius.

3.8.3   **de vindicta, de sanguine** essentially abls. of instrument; the *de* is fairly superfluous. They refer, of course, to Lucius in their talk of revenge and blood.

3.8.4   **parvuli huius in primis annis destituti** talking of the baby in the younger woman's arms, who is now deprived of its father's protection

    legibus vestris et disciplinae publicae litate "make atonement to (i.e., satisfy) your laws and the public order" *Lito* takes the dat. of the person or body that needs propitiating.

3.9.5–3.11.6 A new turn of events

Torture instruments have been brought out and Lucius is bemoaning his fate, when one of the women suggests that before he is tortured, Lucius should look at the bodies of the youths he has slaughtered.

3.9.5   **adplauditur** impers. pass., historic pres.: "there was applause"

3.9.6   **reluctantem me ac diu rennuentem** object of *compellunt*

ostensione apparently an Apuleian word: "by showing"

quam instantissime *quam* + superl. = "as _____ as possible"

manum ipsam de regione lateris trudentes in exitium suum super ipsa cadavera "pushing my hand away from my side over the very cadavers, toward its own destruction," i.e., by lifting the covering off the cadavers, his hand will further its own, and his, destruction.

3.9.7   **ingratis licet** *licet,* when it has the meaning "although," follows the word it governs.

3.9.8   **in peculio Proserpinae et Orci familia numeratus** The image is one of slavery; Lucius had almost become a slave of Proserpina (Persephone) and one of the domestics of Orcus, god of the Underworld.

in contrariam faciem obstupefactus haesi "I stood there dumbfounded at this new (opposite) look of things." Apuleius' use of *in* + acc. is anomalous and often appears where Classical Latin would use the abl. See further below on 3.10: *fixus in lapidem* and 3.21, *in avem sese plumaturam esse.*

novae illius imaginis rationem "the reason for this new appearance (of things)." As Lucius' world falls apart, he grasps for a *ratio* to explain the rather irrational appearance of the world.

3.9.9   **tres utres inflati** The "cadavers" turn out to be wineskins or leather bags made for carrying liquids like wine or oil. *Utres* are also sometimes inflated to use as floating devices. The

Hypatans are never given any explanation for their appearance, though Fotis later tells Lucius that her mistress was in love with a Boeotian youth and had sent the maidservant out to gather some of his hair at a barber shop so that she could cast a spell on him. Fotis was chased away and instead brought home the hairs cut from some wineskins she found nearby. When the mistress casts her spell, it is the wineskins that desperately want to enter the house rather than the youth.

his locis hiantes, quibus illos latrones vulneraveram "gaping in those places in which I had wounded those (the?) robbers." Lucius can't seem to let go of the idea that they were robbers. *Illos* is a weak demonstrative, perhaps more like a definite article; see Introduction, "Style."

3.10.1 **ille quorundam astu paulisper cohibitus risus** "the laughter of some people who had for a while restrained it by guile (*astu*)"; *quorundam* (from *quidam*) is better construed with *risus* than with *astu*.

gratulari, sedare historical infinitives. *gratulari* has sometimes been emended to *graculari*, "to cackle," but *gratulari* makes sense either in its meaning "to give thanks" (to the god Risus) or "to rejoice."

theatro facessunt *theatro* is abl. of separation without a prep.

3.10.2 **laciniam** i.e., the coverlet over the cadavers

fixus in lapidem another innovative use of *in* + acc. This use of *in* often accompanies metamorphosis or change more generally, and may be a deliberate manipulation by Apuleius of a colloquial usage. Here Apuleius combines the idea of "transformed into stone" with "fixed in stone," making use of the idea of motion and change inherent in the construction of *in* with acc. See below on 3.21.

3.10.3 **prius . . . quam** *tmesis*

Milon = *Milo* (nom.)

iniecta manu cf. above on *immissa manu*, but here used without a strict legal meaning

3.10.5   **indignationem iniuriae** objective gen.: "resentment at the wrong done me"

3.11.1   **ecce** not a meaningless particle, but a signal that a surprising shift is about to take place

ipsi magistratus cum suis insignibus Throughout the Festival of Laughter, the magistrates and the apparatus of Roman justice are very much before our eyes; cf. the *lictores duo* who lay hold of Lucius at 3.2. The *insignia* accompanying them are probably the *fasces*, the rods (and usually an axe) carried by the lictors, which symbolize not only their own power to inflict punishment, but the power of the magistrates whom they accompany. There is an interesting contrast between the surreal fiction of the Festival of Laughter and the explicit reality of the legal system. Some have seen here a criticism or at least a parody of the system of justice imposed by Rome on its Greek (and other) provinces.

tuorum "of your family." Notice the way that the magistrates, who speak rather formally, are careful to take note of Lucius' rank and ancestry and he, in his response, first praises the unparalleled splendor of Hypata, a glimpse into some ancient etiquette.

provinciam totam In Apuleius' time, Thessaly was part of the province of Macedonia under Roman rule. Most translators assume a more general meaning and render, "all of Thessaly." At 5.15.4, *provincia* seems to mean "region" generally, and that is probably the meaning here (with thanks to Luca Graverini for the reference).

conplectitur The nobility of Lucius' family "embraces" all of the region, i.e., it has spread through the whole region.

3.11.2   **ne** i.e., *ne . . . quidem*

tristitudinem and later *reverticula* (3.11.3), not found before Apuleius, therefore perhaps neologisms, invented by him

3.11.3   **deo Risui** At the end of Book 2, Lucius' aunt, Byrrhaena, had informed him that the Hypatans, alone of all mortals, worship the god Risus in an annual festival. Nothing is known of this festival outside of Apuleius, and it is assumed that it is his fictional invention, though Plutarch does mention a cult of Gelos (Laughter) at Sparta while discussing several deified abstractions (*Lycurgus* 25, *Cleomenes* 9).

commenti novitate florescit "blossoms through novelty of invention," i.e., every year the city finds some new way to celebrate the Festival of Laughter.

3.11.4 **auctorem et actorem suum** "the originator and performer." Lucius has both (unintentionally) devised the humorous situation and been the primary actor. (This phrase, incidentally, is the origin of the title of Winkler's seminal book on Apuleius, *Auctor and Actor*, in which he looks at the disjunction between the narrating and the experiencing "I" in the work.)

nec patietur ut doleas "he will not allow you to be sad"; *patior* normally takes an infinitive construction.

laetabit act. form (vs. the more common *laetor*); rare and archaic

3.11.5 **patronum scribsit** sc. *te*; "has enrolled you as a patron"; *scribsit = scripsit*

ut in aere stet i.e., as a bronze statue

3.11.6 **sermonis vicem refero** "I reply"

tibi . . . gratiam memini *tibi* is best taken with *gratiam memini* and *splendidissima . . . civitas* as a vocative, where *civitas* has the meaning of "citizens of a state" rather than "state."

parem gratiam memini i.e., *gratiam agere*. We might render as "thanks just the same."

verum "but"

dignioribus meique maioribus "those more worthy and greater than me." If we adopt this reading, *mei* is a gen. of comparison, a grammatical form that appears in later Latin, including other passages in Apuleius. Lucius' polite rejection of the magistrates' offer reflects his general sense of humiliation and disquiet over being the butt of laughter for the entire community. We can assume that he is far from delighted to hear that the god Laughter will now follow him everywhere, even if he is given assurances that it will be *amanter*. This bizarre and disturbing scene does not appear in the pseudo-Lucianic *Onos* and is probably entirely an invention of Apuleius'. (Fellini renders the disquieting and surreal nature of the episode vividly in a scene of his *Satiricon*.) Travelling on business and in search of new adventures, Lucius suddenly finds himself a scapegoat, cruelly used by the Hypatans as a figure of ridicule. At the end of 3.10, Lucius feels utterly humiliated and cannot be consoled for the *indignatio iniuriae* deep in his heart. While the Hypatan magistrates call Risus "gratissimus" and claim that he will drive sadness from Lucius' soul, Lucius does not seem convinced and is still *maestus* at 3.13. Laughter in the *Metamorphoses* is often dark and sadistic; at 2.31, a guest at Byrrhaena's house, Thelyphron, had told a story about his disfigurement by witches, and was met with the *cachinnus* (derisive laughter) of the drunken guests. While Lucius did, in fact, kill the wineskins, there nonetheless seems something arbitrary about his being made a figure of fun, which links the Festival of Laughter to the larger theme of the capriciousness and cruelty of Fortune, which we see in later books. In any case, it is one of the more striking examples of the way Lucius' world is becoming less and less comprehensible and more and more out of his control.

3.21.1–3.22.5 The first metamorphosis

After the Festival of Laughter, Fotis feels remorse because she was indirectly responsible for Lucius' humiliation (see above on 3.9), so, as compensation, Lucius begs her to show him her mistress engaged in magic. Here Fotis calls him to witness a magical event.

3.21.1 **percita Fotis ac satis trepida** i.e., *Fotis percita ac satis trepida*
nihil . . . in suos amores ceteris artibus promoveret "she (Pamphile) was making no progress in her love affair by other

means." *Amores* is regularly used in the pl. to indicate the object of love, here presumably referring to the Boeotian youth whose hair she had demanded earlier when Fotis returned with the hair from the skins which then invaded Milo's house.

in avem sese plumaturam (esse) See above on 3.9 *in contrariam faciem* and 3.10 *fixus in lapidem*. Pamphile will "feather herself into a bird," i.e., turn into a bird.

suum cupitum the one she desired, her beloved

3.21.2 **praepararem** sc. *hortata est ut. . . praepararem;* the indirect statement construction now includes an indirect command with commanding verb and *ut* elided.

3.21.3 **primam noctis vigiliam** The night was divided into four "watches," i.e., intervals for keeping watch, of equal length, which will vary according to the time of year. The first watch is obviously early in the night.

suspenso . . . vestigio i.e., on tiptoe (with my footstep raised up)

quampiam from *quispiam*, "some" or just "a"

sic i.e., as follows in the next section

3.21.4 **iam primum . . . quatit** Only one pple. (*conlocuta*) in this long sentence agrees with Pamphile and the rest belong to a series of abl. absolutes.

omnibus laciniis se devestit Pamphile *devestire* + abl., Pamphile unclothed herself from her garments or took off her clothes.

arcula, pyxides The *arca* is a small chest often used by women to store cosmetics. Here various magical unguents are stored inside in *pyxides* (a Greek word meaning "small wooden boxes").

inde, indidem both mean "from it"

de quis = *de quibus*

ab imis unguibus "from the tips of her toenails"

multumque cum lucerna secreto conlocuta Pamphile talks with her lamp; she had consulted her lamp at dinner in Lucius'

presence at 2.11 and concluded that it would rain. Milo ridi-
cules her for her faith in the prophetic powers of the lamp, re-
minding us that not everyone in antiquity believed in magic.

membra tremulo succussu quatit "she began to shake her
limbs (arms) in a quivering tremor" (Hanson)

3.21.5 **quis** = *quibus* (as above)

crescunt et *et crescunt*

duratur nasus incurvus "her nose curved and hardened," ex-
pressed in Latin by an adj. and a verb

coguntur ungues adunci Her fingers and hands are "com-
pressed" into hooked talons. Note the repetition of *un* sounds,
perhaps suggestive of magical spells.

3.21.6 **bubo** The particular owl into which Pamphile changes is per-
haps the horned owl, considered a funereal bird of ill-omen,
whose cry is is like a querulous groan.

sui periclitabunda "testing herself out." *Periclitabundus* is
constructed with the gen. of the pron., *sui.* Pamphile first
jumps up in the air a little bit before flying off *totis alis,* on
full wing.

3.22.1 **magnis suis artibus** Many editors emend to *magicis,* but *mag-
nis* is the reading of F and is actually more pointed: Pamphile
is possessed of powerful arts while Lucius is rendered power-
less.

praesentis facti stupore "amazement at the deed at hand."
Stupor is constructed with the gen. here.

tantum defixus *tantum* introduces a result clause where *ut* is
omitted (*tantum defixus (ut) quidvis . . .*) Apuleius uses sev-
eral constructions in this section that seem like result clauses
without the *ut*; *sic* and *adeo* below, which could introduce re-
sult clauses, do not seem to imply a correlative *ut.*

quidvis aliud Note the n.; "any*thing* other than Lucius."

3.22.2 **sic exterminatus animi** *exterminatus* is not construed with
the gen. before Apuleius, and commentators have suggested

that *animi* is an original locative, but evidently Apuleius uses the idea of *terminus* in the gen. construction with *exterminatus*: "outside the limits of my mind."

attonitus in amentiam Neither van der Paardt's "struck dumb" nor Turpin's "frightened out of my wits" seems quite the point here. Lucius is so shocked at having witnessed Pamphile's metamorphosis into a bird that he is "shocked into insanity," has no idea who or where he is, feels as if he is dreaming, and has entered a state of complete disorientation. Note Apuleius' vivid use of *in* to describe entering into an abstract state.

adeo *adeo* is probably best taken to mean "and so" as at 8.23, rather than being construed closely with *diu* (*adeo diu*) as an intensive, and rather than as a correlative without the following *ut* (as is *tantum* above).

an vigilarem indirect question, introduced with *an*

3.22.3 **tandem denique** a pleonasm; both words essentially mean "at last; " cf. *ergo igitur* which appears frequently in Apuleius.

admotā still part of the abl. absolute

3.22.4 A crucial moment: Lucius begs Fotis for some of the magic unguent that transformed Pamphile into a bird. He uses all his rhetorical persuasive powers, virtually praying to her and vowing to be her slave forever if she grants his wish.

patere ... perfrui the construction is: *patere* (imperative!) *me fructu perfrui* (*perfrui* is infinitive, taking the abl.).

3.22.5 **impertire** again imperative

nobis "to me"; pl. for sing. within a rather formal context, here implying deference

unctulum indidem i.e., some of that same ointment

unctulum, papillas, mellitula Note the string of diminutives. Lucius plays on their intimacy in a bid to win her over.

tuum mancipium tibi pignera "bind your slave to yourself," a reversal since legally Fotis is the slave. Lucius uses imagery from love poetry where the lover is subjected to his mistress, but the scene also plays into the slave imagery so prevalent in the *Metamorphoses*. See Introduction.

Cupido pinnatus adsistam tibi "(that) I stand by you, my Venus, as winged Cupid," playing on the imagery of the wings he hopes to acquire

3.24 The second metamorphosis

In the intervening sections, Lucius persuades Fotis to procure the magical ointment for him. She creeps into her mistress' room to get it.

3.24.1 **haec adseverans** *haec* refers to Fotis' assurance that it will be easy to transform back into a man by drinking a simple potion of anise and laurel.

3.24.2 **quam** i.e., *pyxidem*. Long sentence; watch the commas to separate clauses.

utque . . . deprecatus indirect command: *deprecatus* ("having prayed") *ut mihi* (dat. with *faveo*) *faveret prosperis volatibus* (abl. of means)

totis = *omnibus*, as often in Apuleius

3.24.3 **alternis conatibus libratis brachiis** "making alternating attempts with my arms stretched out/horizontal." Lucius is flapping his "wings" like a bird. *Librare* is used of the balanced wings of birds in flight. The "alternating" attempts are probably the up-and-down motion.

in avem similem gestiebam The reading is uncertain; many have emended to *similis*. If we retain *similem*, the meaning is that Lucius was trying to turn into a "similar bird," like Pamphile. Also, does *gestio* here mean "I desired" or "I was gesturing?" Since Lucius is flapping his arms up and down in the hopes of transforming into a bird and flying away, the idea seems to be that he was "gesturing" his way into birdhood (he hoped).

nec ullae Supply a verb like "appeared."

3.24.4   Something goes wrong

pili . . . setas/cutis . . . corium The contrasts are clearly between human and animal hair and skin.

in extimis palmulis "at the outer edges of my palms." Perhaps Lucius also refers to his feet, but *palmulae* does not elsewhere refer to feet.

coguntur in singulas ungulas See above on 3.21.5 where Pamphile's hands are similarly compressed and reshaped. In general, Lucius' transformation echoes that of Pamphile, at times ironically.

3.24.5   **sic et aures immodicis horripilant auctibus** "my ears grow hairy with immoderate growth," i.e., my ears grew in the extreme and became hairy. Lucius particularly emphasizes the growth of his ears and male member, two prominent features of the ass and important to the story: in later books, Lucius overhears stories with his capacious ears and also has sexual adventures.

3.24.6   **quod** "the fact that"

mihi nequeunti tenere Photidem "of me no longer able to hold Fotis (in an embrace)"; dat. of advantage or possession. Lucius is simply happy that his male member has grown, not that he will be unable to "hold" Fotis.

natura his private parts, a euphemism

3.25–26 The reactions of Lucius, Fotis, and the pack animals

3.25.1   **salutis inopia** i.e., in a state of utter lack of resource, helplessly; *inopia* is perhaps best taken as abl. of manner without *cum*.

cuncta corporis mei "all of my body"

querens . . . expostulabam Deprived of his voice, one of the main markers of humanity, Lucius still tries to express himself and describes his gestures and thoughts in human terms.

Cf. Ovid's description of Io's frustrations with communication in *Metamorphoses* 1.635–50 after she is transformed into a cow and writes her short name in the earth. See also below on 11.13.

oblicum "sidelong, obliquely," n. used as adv.

3.25.2   **quae** Fotis

3.25.3   **sed bene (est)** "but all is well"

facilior compar.: "quite easy," though this turns out not to be true

rosis tantum demorsicatis "simply by nibbling roses"

exibis asinum Notice the image here; Lucius is still somewhere inside the ass. See below, 3.26.1: *sensum tamen retinebam humanum*

postliminio *Postliminium* is literally the recovery of rights and property by a Roman after exile or captivity, but it seems to have lost its technical force in Apuleius and means simply "back again." On the other hand, it is appropriate because Lucius, when re-transformed, will recover his rights as a human.

3.25.4   **de more** "as is my habit, according to my custom"

ne patereris negative purpose clause: "so that you would not have to suffer"

Now that Lucius is an ass, he goes off dejectedly to the stable to join his horse and Milo's other ass. Lucius grapples here with his new identity and with the task of deciphering how animals think.

3.26.1   **perfectus** past pple. of *perficio* more strongly than the adjectival *perfectus*.

3.26.2   **deliberavi** Van der Paardt (1971) points out the parallel to Odysseus' deliberations over whether to kill the Cyclops in *Odyssey* 9—until he realizes that they need the Cyclops to move the boulder that blocks the exit.

nequissimam facinerosissimamque . . . spissis Note the alliteration of *s*, expressing Lucius' sudden hatred of Fotis.

3.26.3   **rursus** here means "in turn, in addition."

3.26.4   **demussata temporali contumelia** "swallowing down the temporary indignity." Like Fotis, Lucius believes that his time as an ass will be short.

durissimo casui meo serviens "enslaved to my very harsh lot" (*servio* + dat.), again the slavery motif

Milonis quondam hospitis mei Now that he is an ass, Lucius is no longer Milo's guest, properly speaking.

alium . . . asinum Lucius here clearly considers himself an ass.

3.26.5   **rebar . . . equum meum praebiturum (esse)** indirect statement

si quod inesset . . . praebiturum esse *quod* is indef. (after *si, nisi, num,* and *ne*): "any." *Inesset* is impf. subjunctive in a conditional clause within indirect discourse introduced by a verb in the past tense: a fut. less vivid condition (A&G 589a3; Bradley's Arnold #471) rather than contrary to fact.

sacramentum Lucius uses a term expressing legal obligation, most familiar as the word for the military oath of allegiance, to describe the instinctive sense of loyalty and obligation he expects from his horse.

loca lautia technical term for the special treatment offered by the Roman Senate to foreign visiting dignitaries. "Special treatment" (Hanson).

3.26.6   **pro Iuppiter hospitalis** Jupiter is regarded as the god of hospitality. *Pro* is an interjection rather than the prep. here.

Fidei secreta numina The point may be that Fides has departed from the earth and hence is *secreta* in the sense of "remote" (van der Paardt), or perhaps the idea is that the principles of Fides are secret, unspoken, unwritten (OLD 6).

praeclarus ille vector meus This time the epithet is sarcastic, like *gratissimo* below, while *probissimum* above expressed genuine praise.

capita conferunt "put their heads together"; the pl. verb conforms to the sense rather than the grammar.

scilicet "evidently"; the particle indicates that Lucius had no way of actually knowing what he reports, but is merely inferring.

3.26.7 **verentes cibariis suis** "fearing for their food," dat. of the thing on behalf of which fear is felt, OLD 3c

vix videre (i.e., **viderunt**) . . . **insecuntur** One expects *cum* or *et:* they had scarcely seen me *when* . . .

insecuntur = *insequuntur*

3.26.8 **quam procul** See above, 2.7.7.

Book 4

4.4–5 On the road with the robbers; the other ass

After Lucius' metamorphosis, a band of robbers invaded Milo's house and stole not only a large amount of money, but also Lucius, his horse, and the other ass. They are now on the road to their lair. In this section, we can observe the way that Lucius assumes characteristics of both human and ass; he insists on his rational capabilities, but has much in common with the other ass.

4.4.1   **nec mora cum** a common Apuleian expression: "there was no delay when" or "immediately"

iam in meridiem prono iubare The phrase is obscure. Normally *meridies* means "noon" or "south," but if the sun is at an angle (*pronus*), it is evidently not noon. At 4.1, it was already *dies media*, so it is now probably afternoon. Commentators suggest that in Apuleius *meridies* can mean "afternoon," so here the phrase would mean "when the sunlight was already sloping downward into the afternoon" or, as commonly understood, "toward setting."

longe gravius onustum "much more heavily burdened"; *longe*, as elsewhere in Apuleius, means "very, very much"

illi latrones This use of *illi* may be part of the shift of forms of *ille* into the Romance languages' definite article or it may be derogatory like *iste*. cf. *illi gratissimo famulo* above, 3.26.

4.4.2   **iamque . . . occumbere** long sentence, but mostly consisting of an uncomplicated string of participial phrases and adjs. with abl. absolutes interspersed

ungulis extritis abl. absolute, "since my hooves had been worn down"

4.4.3   **rivulum quendam propter insistens** i.e., *propter rivulum quendam insistens* (anastrophe)

scite "ingeniously." Note the irony.

4.4.4   **certus atque obstinatus** with infinitive: "bound and deter-
mined (not to get up)"

ingrediundum archaic for *ingrediendum*

**paratus non fusti tantum sed machaera perfossus occum-
bere** "prepared to lie there (die?) dug into not only by a cud-
gel, but by a sword." The phrase is problematic: *perfossus*
has seemed to some an inappropriate word for the action of
a cudgel or club (*fustis*), used more for beating, and the text
is sometimes emended to add *percussus* ("beaten") after *tan-
tum*, but the text will work as it stands. *Occumbere*, if it means
"die" is not only inconsistent with Lucius' actions in the next
section, but also with the substance of his clever plan to lie
down and refuse to go on and be granted a *causaria missio*.
Hanson in the Loeb translates *occumbere* "lie there" which is
a rare, but possible meaning for the word.

4.4.5   **causariam missionem** technical term for a medical discharge
from the army; note the characteristic Latin use of military
imagery.

latrones . . . distributuros . . . relicturos (esse) continuing
indirect statement dependent on *rebar*

in altioris vindictae vicem "instead of a greater punishment";
in vicem often means "in place of."

4.5.1–4   **namque . . . praecipitant** another very long sentence. Take a
break at *quoad* where the subject changes from the other ass
to the robbers.

4.5.2   **iacensque in mortuum** If the reading is correct, this is yet an-
other example of *in* with acc. expressing metamorphosis. The
other ass is lying there "as if dead," but is also transforming
into a dead ass, as it turns out.

ne . . . elevatis long abl. absolute; *ne* is equivalent to *ne . . .
quidem*; see 3.11.

4.5.3   **postumae spei fatigati** The subject is now the robbers, but
the phrase is obscure. Hanson translates "tired of waiting for
posthumous success," in other words, frustrated by the fact

that, at this rate, the realization of their hopes would come after their deaths.

ne . . . morarentur negative purpose clause

mortuo immo vero lapideo asino servientes *servio* takes the dat., here meaning "tending to, accommodating"; *immo vero* slightly corrects *mortuo*.

4.5.4   **per altissimum praeceps** *praeceps* is a n. noun here.

retractum, spirantem pples. referring to the other ass

4.5.5   **asinum bonae frugi** *bonae frugi* is a common predicate dat. phrase meaning "virtuous, honest, sober." Lucius decides to be a good, honest ass.

4.5.6   **nam et . . . habitatio** The strongly paratactic and randomly unfolding details of this sentence give the sense of Lucius catching phrases here and there spoken by the robbers. The use of *quod* (see below) to introduce an indirect statement may likewise represent a colloquial tone in the robbers' language.

quod esset habenda mansio *quod* here introduces indirect discourse with the subjunctive, as it begins to do in later Latin (Callebat 338–39). *Mansio* is abstract here, a stop; the robbers were saying that they would shortly have to make a stop.

in proximo "close at hand"

4.5.7   **clementi transmisso clivulo** Here the description of the landscape obviously mirrors Lucius' more optimistic mental state.

vice lavacri "in place of a bath," one of the more interesting examples of Lucius' position between human and animal

4.28.1–4.30.3 The tale of Cupid and Psyche begins

The tale of Cupid and Psyche (4.28–6.24) is the best-known portion of the *Metamorphoses*, often excerpted or treated as a myth in the public sphere without reference to its Apuleian authorship. From the end of Book 4 to near the end of Book 6, Lucius' adventures are interrupted by this long tale, the longest of the "embedded tales" in the novel. For a more thorough discussion of this most famous section of Apuleius' works, see the Introduction.

In the intervening chapters, the robbers have arrived at their base, and soon another contingent arrives with a young girl whom they have taken captive. The girl, Charite, laments having been taken captive right in the midst of her wedding. She is comforted by an old woman who cooks and cares for the robbers and who tells her a long tale as a distraction.

The tale begins with a description of the effects of Psyche's superhuman beauty, which has much in common with the indescribable beauty of the heroines of ideal romance (see Introduction). She is so beautiful that mortals mistake her for Venus and worship her with rites that properly belong to the goddess—which enrages Venus.

Fig. 2 Cupid and Psyche by Antonio Canova, 1796. Louvre, Paris. Réunion des Musées Nationaux / Art Resource, NY.

4.28.1 Note the folktale beginning; a "once upon a time" story is clearly commencing. We have entered another world, of kings and queens and princesses, as well as talking ants and wise towers—far from the land of magic and robbers within which it is told.

habuere = *habuerunt*

numero, forma, natu abls. of respect

quamvis . . . tamen Note the opposition of the two clauses.

gratissima specie abl. of description

maiores . . . natu . . . celebrari posse . . . credebantur The elder sisters (*maiores natu,* abl. supine) are the subject of *credebantur.*

quidem emphasizing *maiores*

4.28.2 **iunioris** "youngest," not simply "younger" (as at 9.37, *e tribus iunior*)

tam praecipua tam praeclara modifying *pulchritudo*; asyndeton—supply *et.*

penuria abl. of cause: "due to the poverty of human speech"

Note the extreme alliteration of *p* in this section. This could be Apuleian baroqueness, though sometimes alliteration of *p* in Latin seems to mimic stuttering (cf.11.14 when Lucius recovers his voice: "*quid potissimum praefarer primarium*").

4.28.3 **multi civium** = *multi cives.* Note the post-Classical use of the partitive gen.

studiosa celebritate "in eager crowds" abl. of manner; abstract for concrete (*celebritas*)

inaccessae formonsitatis admiratione stupidi "struck dumb with admiration of her unparalleled beauty." *Stupidi* modifies the phrase *multi . . . civium.*

priore digito in erectum pollicem residente "with fingertip resting on their raised thumb"; abl. absolute; the gesture is apparently one of admiration, either religious or secular. One might compare the gesture stereotypically made by chefs admiring their creations (Kenney).

ut deam Venerem venerabantur *ut* with indicative: "as"

4.28.4   **proximas civitates . . . regiones** direct objects of *pervaserat*

deam . . . conversari indirect discourse after *fama pervaserat*: "that the goddess was mingling"

quam caerulum profundum pelagi peperit According to the Greek poet Hesiod (*Theogony* 195–97), Aphrodite (the Greek version of Venus) was born from the castrated genitals of Uranos, which his son Cronos had thrown into the sea. She arose from the foam (*aphros*) that formed on the surface of the water.

ros spumantium fluctuum "the water of the foaming waves." The language plays on the etymology of the name Aphrodite (see above), even though the goddess is called "Venus" in Latin.

numinis sui passim tributa venia abl. absolute: "the favor of her divine power granted broadly"; i.e., they thought that Venus was spreading herself and her power among humans.

vel certe practically the start of a new sentence

non maria sed terras . . . pullulasse continuing the indirect discourse of above

novo . . . germine "from a new sprouting of heavenly drops," referring obliquely to the birth of Venus

4.29.1   **immensum** adv.; "enormously." Note the extreme alliteration of *p* here, but this time perhaps reflecting the bubbling of the spreading gossip.

opinio i.e., the belief that the girl (Psyche) was Venus incarnate

insulas . . . plurimas all direct objects of *pervagatur* (cf. above at 28.4)

terrae plusculum *plusculum* is substantive; "a large part of the earth."

fama porrecta abl. absolute

4.29   The following sentences describe Venus' cult in decline. Before Psyche usurped her honors, Venus' shrine would have been flocked with worshippers offering her the sacrifice of animals on her altars (most often small animals like pigs), and communal meals would have followed. Bones and fat from the animals were burned in offering to the goddess. Her worshippers would have prayed to her for aid and protection in front of the shrine and would have crowned her cult image within the shrine with flowers. Apuleius also mentions the Roman custom of the *lectisternium*, a banquet offered to and in honor of the gods, at which portable cult images of deities were placed on couches (*pulvinaria*). See Beard, North, and Price, I, 39–40; II, 130–31.

4.29.3   **altimissimis. . . meatibus** "over the deepest paths of the sea"

Paphon, Cnidon, Cythera accs. of place to which; the first two are Greek accs. All three are known for their shrines of Venus; Cythera is the goddess' birthplace.

nemo . . . nemo . . . navigabant The two *nemo*'s are constructed with a pl. verb.

pulvinaria proteruntur See note above on the *lectisternium*.

incoronata, foedatae Supply *sunt*.

viduae The altars are "bereft," an odd sort of personification.

frigido cinere because no animal offerings were being burned

4.29.4   **supplicatur** impers. (with dat.), historic pres.,"supplication was made," i.e., people supplicated

victimis et epulis i.e., with sacrificial animals and ceremonial meals

commeantem "as she (Psyche) went back and forth"

floribus sertis et solutis flowers woven into garlands and loose

4.29.5   **impatiens indignationis** i.e., Venus could not repress her anger, but spoke out.

4.30   Venus' outraged speech is particulary indebted to Lucretius and Vergil. Lucretius' epic about the natural world (evoked here) begins with a proem praising Venus as the creative principle (and goes on to explain the science of the world in Epicurean terms). The Vergilian reminiscences here and elsewhere characterize Venus as Juno of the *Aeneid*—angry and vindictive. At the same time, Venus' language here sets up her opposition to the goddess, Isis, who introduces herself with the words "*en adsum . . . rerum naturae parens, elementorum omnium domina, saeculorum progenies initialis*" (11.5).

4.30.1 **En . . . en . . . en** a series of angry and sarcastic exclamations. The particle *en* should be translated accordingly.

rerum naturae . . . alma Venus allusions to Lucretius. The probable title of his epic is *De Rerum Natura*, a phrase that appears in Lucretius' epic at 1.21 and 25. In line 2, Venus is called "*alma Venus.*" Venus is being sarcastic here, of course, and Lucretius' epic becomes the standard for measuring the honor Venus should be receiving.

elementorum also a Lucretian word, but here it means "elements" (land, sea, and air) rather than "atoms" as it would in Lucretius.

orbis totius alma Venus *alma* is used substantively with the gen.: "nourisher, mother"; see OLD *almus* b; Kenney 122.

partiario maiestatis honore tractor "I am treated/dealt with by having to share the honor due to my majesty . . . " *Tractor* probably means "I am treated" rather than "I am dragged in the dust."

4.30.2 **vicariae venerationis incertum** *incertum* is a substantive: "the uncertainty of substitute worship."

moritura In other words, Psyche is a mortal, but the word also sounds like a threat.

4.30.3 **pastor ille** i.e., Paris, who had awarded Venus the golden apple as the most beautiful goddess (Juno and Minerva being the rivals), in exchange for which she gave him Helen, precipitating the Trojan War. Venus' complaints evoke Juno's anger at Paris (*Aeneid* 1.37–49) for having slighted her beauty when he chose Venus.

cuius iustitiam . . . magnus comprobavit Iuppiter Jupiter had appointed Paris as judge, but there is an irony in the reference to *iustitia* and *fides* since Paris decided the contest by accepting a bribe.

non adeo gaudens use of a Greek construction—*ou chairousa*—"she will not happily have usurped." This is combined with the Latin expression *non adeo*, "not so much," an understatement.

faxo archaic for *fecero*, here used with the subjunctive: "I'll make sure . . . "

paeniteat the usual impers. construction with gen. of the cause of regret. (A&G 354 b and c)

Book 5

5.11.3–4 Psyche's husband warns her yet again not to listen to her sisters

In the intervening portion, 4.32–5.11, we hear that Psyche is so beautiful that no mortal man dares to court her, so her parents consult the oracle of Apollo at Miletus, who tells them to leave her on a rocky crag dressed for her marriage to some fearsome snake-like creature. Psyche is swept up by a soft Zephyr and wafted to a magical gem-studded palace where she is waited on by disembodied voices and invisible servants. At night, her unknown husband visits her and makes her his wife, but demands that she not look at him. He leaves in the morning and returns every night and Psyche is relatively happy, but lonely. Soon, her sisters search her out and visit her and, jealously realizing that her husband is divine, with all evil intent, convince her to look at her husband, reminding her that the oracle said he would be a serpent.

5.11.3 **velitatur . . . eminus . . . comminus** military language. Fortune is "skirmishing" at a distance, but will soon engage in hand-to-hand combat.

longe = *valde* (with *firmiter*)

5.11.4 **lupulae** Referring to the sisters, the word is an Apuleian invention, a diminutive of *lupa*, "wolf," with its derogatory slang meaning, "prostitute."

vultus poetic pl., as often

non videbis si videris typical Apuleian wordplay expressing via a paradox that, if Psyche looks at her husband, he will have to leave her. He adds that Psyche is now pregnant and that the child will be divine if she obeys his injunction not to look at him, but if she disobeys, mortal.

5.22–23 Psyche's sisters advise her

The sisters reappear and this time convince Psyche that her husband is a monster who is just waiting until she is fat with her unborn child to devour them both—therefore she must arm herself and kill the monster.

5.22.1 **alioquin** The word means "as a general rule," contrasting Psyche's usual passive state with her current boldness. This is a favorite Apuleian word, which, like that other Apuleian favorite, *prorsus*, is often hard to translate.

et corporis et animi gens. of specification depending on *infirma* (A&G 349d)

fati saevitia subministrante a differently phrased reference to *saeva Fortuna*, who hounds Lucius and Psyche. Here Fate is only represented as aiding Psyche in carrying out her ill-advised plan.

sexum audacia mutatur Grammatically, either *mutatur* is pass. and *sexum* is an acc. of respect, or *mutatur* is middle ("she changes") and *sexum* is the direct object. While this phrase mainly presents Psyche as "manly" because she is daring a brave deed worthy of a male, it points to a widespread deconstructing of gender and gender roles in the *Metamophoses*. In this episode, Cupid is portrayed as rather androgynous (soft and delicate; see below), but the tales of the robbers also involve men dressing as women and vice versa. In the current tale, women assume nearly all the roles: narrator, addressee, goddess antagonist, protagonist. See above on 1.2 and the general Introduction.

5.22.2 **omnium ferarum mitissimam dulcissimamque bestiam** The phrase itself gradually domesticates the "beast," moving from *fera* through superls. of gentleness to *bestia* and thus redefining the "beast" of oracle and of the sisters' imagination.

Cupidinem The climactic moment has arrived. Psyche discovers that her husband is Cupid, not a monster. She has been remarkably naïve about his identity—couldn't she feel his wings at least?—but would the ancient reader have known all along? The answer to this question is bound up with the question of what exactly Apuleius' role is in shaping this story. How much did he invent? What already existed? What we can observe is the way he has tried to build suspense, not allowing the omniscient narrator to let anything slip, trying to deceive us with false leads; it is not until several pages later that Venus herself learns the truth about Cupid's lover, for example, and the Milesian oracle had called Psyche's husband a *vipereum malum*.

acuminis sacrilegi novacula praenitebat This is the reading of F defended by the Groningen commentaries; the knife is lit up by the flaring of the lamp. *Acuminis sacrilegi* is gen. of quality or description: "the knife with its sharp point." Most editors emend to *acuminis sacrilegi novaculam paenitebat*: "the knife repented of its sharp point," which is attractive, but not necessary. We hear later about the knife's moral qualities. *Praenitebat* adds to the emphasis on light and shining in the description of Cupid.

5.22.3   **marcido pallore defecta** The abl. is better taken as descriptive rather than causal, so "weakened and with a fainting pallor" rather than "overcome *by* a fainting pallor."

desedit in imos poplites "she sank back onto the back of her knees"; i.e., she fell back into a crouching position with her knees bent.

sed in suo pectore As GCA points out, this is the first of five suicide attempts by Psyche in the episode, which not only recalls the heroines (and more often heroes) of Greek romance, but also characterizes her. The *sed* seems to mark a correction in the gesture of Psyche; she begins to hide the knife, but then aims it at her own breast.

5.22.4   **fecisset . . . nisi . . . evolasset** past contrary to fact

timore tanti flagitii The knife, like other objects in the "Tale of Cupid and Psyche" is personified. The "crime" would be the injuring of Cupid's bride.

salute defecta "left without salvation"; see OLD *deficio* 2a for the pass. with an abl.

recreatur animi *recreo* (pass. in middle sense) here takes a gen.

5.22.5 **videt** Notice the verb at the beginning of the sentence (similarly *videt* appears first in its clause at 5.22.2), emphasizing Psyche's act of seeing, and clearing the way for the lush description that follows.

genialem All the various meanings of *genialis* seem to come together here—"joyous," "pleasing," and "nuptial," perhaps especially the last since Psyche's reaction is a sensual one.

caesariem Critics have often noted that Lucius (or possibly Apuleius since it seems to extend beyond the *Met.*) has a hair fetish. This appears most strikingly at 2.8–9 where Lucius admires Fotis' hair and digresses on all the amazing varieties of hair in general.

ambrosia temulentam Here (as elsewhere) ambrosia is not the food of the gods, but rather a divine unguent or perfume. The hair is "drunk" with it.

cervices object of *pererrantes*. The pl. used for sing. seems to be the original form; hence Apuleius is, as often, archaizing.

decoriter impeditos *decoriter* first appears here. Cupid seems to be wearing a band around his head, but his abundant locks are still all over the place.

splendore nimio fulgurante probably best taken as abl. of cause

splendore . . . vacillabat The idea is that Cupid's hair is so divinely luminescent that even the actual light (*ipsum lumen*) falters in the presence of this great brilliance.

roscidae literally "dewy," suggesting morning freshness and more brightness

5.22.6 **micanti flore** *flos* here is figurative.

plumulae tenellae double diminutive emphasizing the downiness and the erotic quality that diminutives can impart; cf. above on Fotis at 2.7 and *glabellum, lectulus* below.

inquieta n. pl. used adverbially: "ceaselessly"

quale peperisse Venerem non paeniteret potential subjunctive of *paeniteo*, impers. verb, here constructed with the infinitive (*peperisse*)

The description of Cupid is, of course, a rhetorical tour de force. How can one possibly describe what the god of love looks like? Apuleius shows off his powers as a writer, inventing words, piling on colors, diminutives, light, slight movement—baroque lushness in general. He also shows us the reactions of the knife, Psyche, and the lamp, which, in a way, tell us more than mere description. Some scholars mention here the connection of the passage to mystery cults; i.e., religious cults in which the non-initiate is forbidden to see the god or know his/her mysteries. Upon initiation, the worshipper has a revelation and looks upon the divinity. Certainly, there is an element of that experience here, an experience that would have been familiar to contemporary readers. Perhaps more strongly, what Psyche and we experience is the sensuality of Cupid. In the following section, Psyche is immediately filled with desire; the lamp (perhaps) wants to kiss Cupid. So, the experience of "seeing god" is overshadowed by a very bodily sensuality.

5.22.7 **propitia tela** a seeming paradox, but reminding us that Cupid's arrows operate for the good

5.23.1 **quae** i.e., *tela*

insatiabili animo Psyche satis et curiosa Psyche's curiosity is an important element in the tale (perhaps, however, overemphasized) and links her with Lucius the curious protagonist. This is the first time the narrator has called her *curiosa*. *Satis* should be translated as "fairly" or "very." Psyche's *curiositas* is paired with her *animus insatiabilis*, which also points ahead to her desire.

rimatur ... mariti ... miratur Note the repetition of sounds.

5.23.2 **punctu pollicis** The reading of F is *puncto*, but *punctu* ("by pricking or stabbing") seems preferable. Various editors interpret *puncto* as "with the point of her thumb," which is, however, an unattested meaning of *punctum* ("hole, pinprick"). GCA defend *puncto* and translate "a prick in her thumb," but this interpretation seems at odds with the result: substantial drops of blood.

5.23.3 **sponte** Although Psyche has been wounded by the arrows of Cupid, her love is nonetheless represented as arising from her own volition.

in Amoris incidit amorem/ cupidine fraglans Cupidinis Apuleian wordplay, but also providing an interesting slippage between the concrete god and his abstraction

prona in eum . . . Commentators point to parallels with erotic elegy in which male elegists watch their sleeping lovers (e.g., Propertius 1.3), but it is also noteworthy that in this female tale the roles are reversed and that the female narrator (narratrix) vividly describes Psyche's desire.

5.23.4 **bono tanto** Some translate *bonum* here as "physical beauty," but more than that is meant—"blessing," perhaps.

saucia mente the language of wounded love; cf. Dido *gravi saucia cura*, (*Aeneid.* 4.1)

lucerna illa *illa* indicates that the lamp has already been mentioned.

5.23.4-5 The lamp is interestingly highlighted and, in this folktale-like episode, given agency and addressed by the narratrix.

evomuit i.e., "spewed, sputtered," but personfication is active

luminis sui "from the end of its spout," an unusual meaning for *lumen* (OLD 8b)

5.23.5 **hem** The particle expresses surprise and indignation and is comic and archaic.

ignis totius deum Cupid is associated with fire in his capacity to burn lovers, but being god of all fire or "fire in its totality" gives him cosmic status and again contrasts him with the humble, earthly lamp that, paradoxically, is burning him.

scilicet The word expresses a presumption on the part of the narrator; cf. 3.26.3, 11.1.3.

5.23.6 **visaque detectae fidei colluvie** "seeing the filth of his betrayed/uncovered trust," a difficult and somewhat disputed phrase. It is his identity that is uncovered, not his trust, but the general sense is clear.

Book 6
6.20–21 Psyche's labors

Psyche has performed several labors in her servitude to Venus, first separating a mound of tiny seeds into discreet categories, next gathering wool from some fierce sheep, then drawing water from a fountain at the top of an inaccessible cliff, aided in all cases by animals who pity her plight and know her as the lover of Cupid. The last labor involves descending to the Underworld to collect a bit of Proserpina's beauty; here she is advised by a speaking tower who gives very specific instructions.

A descent to the Underworld, or *katabasis,* is a feature of epic. Odysseus and Aeneas made well-known descents in their respective epics. Psyche's *katabasis* is filled with folktale and specifically female elements: advice from a speaking tower, specific prohibitions, a visit to the queen of the Underworld and a quest to bring back her beauty. These are quite distinct from Hercules' valiant labors or Aeneas' descent to gain a vision of the future greatness of Rome and to hear instructions on how to effect its foundation. Yet Apuleius borrows language extensively from Vergil for his description of the Underworld (earlier in Book 6). Perhaps we may read the adoption of epic language as comic, or perhaps Psyche's journey can be seen as a novelistic version of a *katabasis.*

6.20.1   **sumptisque rite stipibus, etc.** The abl. absolutes refer to the enactment of advice given earlier by the tower.

6.20.2   **asinario debili** Interestingly, Psyche encounters a lame ass and lame driver in the Underworld, as if a surrogate Lucius had somehow accompanied her. In a sense, then, Lucius, too, has his *katabasis.*

supernatantis mortui . . . textricum subdolis Psyche is advised to ignore the pleas of a floating dead man and the requests for help by old women weaving, apparently traps set by Venus to make Psyche drop one of the barley-cakes necessary to feed Cerberus to secure her exit.

sopita canis horrenda rabie *canis* is gen.: "the horrifying madness of the dog (having been) lulled to sleep"

domum Proserpinae The old woman narrator refers to the house by its mistress' name.

6.20.3 **humilis** agreeing with (understood) Psyche

cibario pane ordinary bread normally given to servants. Throughout this scene, Psyche humbles herself and acts more like a slave or servant than a guest, as the tower had advised.

6.20.4 **repletam conclusamque** by Proserpina

offulae sequentis fraude "by the beguilement of the second cake" (Purser)

6.20.5 **mentem capitur** acc. of respect: she was overcome in her mind.

curiositate cf. Psyche's earlier curiosity about her lover's identity

6.20.6 **vel sic** *vel* has the meaning "possibly" here. Psyche reveals insecurity about her ability to please Cupid, the idea being that possibly, by taking some of the divine beauty, she will succeed in this way (*sic*).

6.21.1 **coperculo revelatus** "uncovered by the lid [being removed]"

crassaque soporis nebula cunctis eius membris perfunditur *cunctis membris* is dat. with *perfunditur*; "a cloud is poured over . . . "

in ipso vestigio, ipsaque semita i.e., exactly where she stood

6.21.2 **dormiens cadaver** The text makes it rather unclear whether Psyche is dead or sleeping. A "truly Stygian" sleep pours over her, yet she ultimately seems more asleep than dead (*sopor* and *somnus* are used to describe her state, yet she is a *cadaver*). There is an element of resurrection and rebirth in the act, which parallels Lucius' physical and spiritual rebirth in Book 11 and is also a feature of the Greek romance.

Psyches Greek gen.

6.21.3   **longe velocius** "much more quickly" (than usual, because he had rested his wings)

curiose here = "carefully," one of the positive uses of the word

innoxio puncto sagittae Normally, of course, the wound of Cupid's arrow induces love, but here it seems merely to wake Psyche from the Stygian sleep. Kenney (1990) suggests that Psyche may wake to a true perception of Love.

6.21.4   **perieras** "you would have perished" (hypothetical indicative)

provinciam . . . exsequere *provincia* means not only a "province," but a task assigned to a magistrate. This latter meaning, with a generalized and humorous sense, applies here (OLD 1b). Cupid advises Psyche to execute the task Venus assigned her.

amator levis in pinnas se dedit Kenney: "her fickle lover," but Cupid is far from fickle here, falling deeply in love with Psyche and committing himself to her. Rather, *levis* may refer to Cupid's lightness as he rises on his wings.

In fact, at this point, Cupid, *amore nimio peresus,* goes to Jupiter and asks him to intercede. After some comic bits about Jupiter's habitual passions for mortal females, the king of the gods agrees to make Psyche immortal and marry her to Cupid.

6.23.5–6.24.4 A wedding banquet among the gods

6.23.5   **iubet** The subject is Jupiter.

ambrosiae One might expect her to drink nectar, which is the drink of the gods (and drunk by Jupiter a few lines later) rather than ambrosia, more often the solid food, but reference to ambrosia as liquid is not unparalleled.

immortalis esto *esto* is the fut. imperative of *sum*, often used in legal contexts. The full phrase used by Jupiter here may recall the legal formula for freeing slaves, *liber esto*, given the evocation of slavery in both Lucius' and Psyche's sufferings.

6.24.1 **summum torum** The gods seem to recline at table like the Romans, and Cupid and Psyche clearly have the place of honor.

sic et . . . i.e., Jupiter was also sitting with Juno. Note that in this nuptial context Juno is referred to as "his" Juno.

6.24.2 **suus pocillator** Ganymede, a beautiful Trojan youth snatched up to the sky to be Jupiter's cupbearer (and lover)

Liber, Vulcanus etc. *Liber* = Bacchus. Vulcan cooks by virtue of his capacity as god of fire, and other gods here perform menial tasks related to their divine powers.

6.24.3 **Horae** As goddesses of the seasons, they are able to make flowers grow.

superingressa i.e., Venus enters the scene after the music has already begun, she "entered upon the music"

scaena sibi sic concinnata The scene was arranged by Venus (*sibi*), in such a way that (*sic . . . ut*—result clause) the Muses, etc. sang and played instruments. The word *scaena* evokes the theatrical elements of the *Metamorphoses,* which can be seen, for example, in the Festival of Laughter, which took place in the theater and was marked by performance and acting. It has been suggested that this scene is indebted to popular mime or pantomime productions, satyr plays and also wall paintings.

Paniscus, Satyrus minor rustic deities playing rustic and plebeian instruments. The mixing of social levels represented by the marriage itself is also seen in the company of the various levels of gods.

6.24.4 **convenit in manum Cupidinis** a technical phrase for the passing of the wife from her father's power into her husband's

filia While the birth of a daughter may be a surprise (Cupid had spoken earlier of the child using the masculine gender, *hoc parvulo,* 5.13), it is fully in keeping with the extremely female-oriented nature of the tale, as well as with the gender of *Voluptas.*

Voluptatem The important question here, debated by scholars, is whether, on a symbolic level, the Pleasure in question is of an earthly or heavenly nature. Does this union of Love and the Soul lead to the attainment of a transcendent Platonic Joy or does the birth of *Voluptas* signify indulgence in sensual pleasures? (See further, general Introduction.)

Thus ends the "Tale of Cupid and Psyche." What is the purpose of this long digression within the *Metamorphoses*? It is worth considering that: (1) all the embedded tales in the *Metamorphoses* are entertaining in themselves and also connect to themes of the whole work and, in one way or another, to the central narrative of Lucius' adventures; (2) the basic trajectory of this tale is that of an expulsion from a human community, to a "fall" because of "curiosity," to subsequent struggles and labors, to reintegration into a new community and a higher state (deification). There are clear echoes here of Lucius' story so far—his departure from home, his curiosity about magic, his sufferings as an ass. For a fuller discussion, see Introduction.

Book 9

9.12.2–9.13.5 Lucius and the slaves in the mill

Books 7, 8, and 9 continue Lucius' travels and sufferings. After the "Tale of Cupid and Psyche," Charite is rescued by her fiancé/husband, Tlepolemus, who infiltrates the band, gets the robbers drunk, ties them up, and brings in the authorities. (Incidentally, the old woman who tells the "Tale of Cupid and Psyche" hangs herself after Charite, riding Lucius, temporarily escapes.) Their story seems to have a happy ending, but, after some intervening adventures, we hear at the beginning of Book 8 that an old suitor, Thrasyllus, kills Tlepolemus on a boar hunt, making it look like the work of the boar. He begins to court Charite, but Tlepolemus' ghost visits her in a dream and reveals the truth (with echoes of Sychaeus' appearance to Dido in *Aeneid* 1). Charite tricks Thrasyllus into coming to her room at night where she gouges out his eyes. She then runs madly through the town (again with echoes of Dido's frenzy from *Aeneid* 4) and kills herself on her husband's tomb. Thrasyllus afterward locks himself in their common tomb and starves himself to death. This tale, in two installments, dominates Books 7 and 8.

Meanwhile, in the frame narrative, after Charite and Lucius are rescued, Lucius is sent out to pasture with some horses and is momentarily happy, eyeing some attractive mares, but is soon set to work carrying wood down from the mountain, under the immediate supervision of a sadistic boy who beats Lucius, heaps stones on top of his already heavy load, and ties thorny branches to his tail. (The boy is later torn apart by a bear.) After the deaths of Charite and Tlepolemus, all the slaves of that household flee, taking Lucius along. They are attacked by wolves and encounter an old man who turns out to be a devouring serpent. Lucius is sold to some charlatan priests of the Syrian Goddess. These priests are later arrested and Lucius is sold to a miller who puts him to work in the mill, turning a wheel to grind grain into flour. He hears various tales of adultery and himself exposes the miller's wife, who has hidden her young lover. The miller makes the boy his own lover instead, and is later (after the following passage) murdered by his wife through witchcraft.

Working in an ancient mill, here attached to a bakery, was one of the most tedious and back-breaking of jobs, assigned to the lowest in the social hierarchy: slaves and animals. Here, given a break, Lucius looks around with curiosity at his fellow sufferers. The passage is remarkable for its uniquely vivid depiction of the plight of slaves in the ancient world.

In this passage, the animals appear to be pushing the mill-wheel around and around in circles, while the slaves are loading in the wheat and unloading flour, though other Latin authors mention slaves turning the mill.

Fig. 3 Urnholder of Publius Nonius Zethus, representing a donkey in a mill, first century CE. Vatican Museum. Wikimedia Commons.

9.12.2   Note the series of adjs. all applied to *ego* (i.e., Lucius): *fatigatus, indiguus, perditus, attonitus, anxius*, creating a semi-rhyming effect

indiguus + *abl.* (*refectione virium*)

prorsus Construe with *perditus*.

familiari curiositate Even in desperate circumstances, Lucius is curious.

postposito cibo abl. absolute

officinae The "workshop" referred to is the mill.

cum delectatione quadam Given the description that follows, it is hard to see why Lucius looks on with a certain pleasure. Kenney (2003) suggests that the pleasure lies in the occasion to exercise his literary skills. It may also be related to the sense that he has gained important knowledge (see below).

9.12.3   **homunculi** The diminutive refers both to the literal size of the men whose growth is stunted and to the worth society assigns them. Note the other diminutives: *centunculo* (7), *tegili* (8), *pannulos* (10).

totam cutem acc. of respect, "their whole skin painted with . . . " Similarly, *dorsumque plagosum* in line 7 and *pubem* in line 9. The slaves have been whipped or beaten.

nonnulli exiguo tegili . . . iniecti *iniecti* with abl.: "covered with"

tegili The word appears only here (*hapax legomenon*).

tantum modo *modo* intensifies *tantum*.

9.12.4   **sic tunicati ut essent** result clause

frontes litterati et capillum semirasi et pedes anulati all signs of slavery. These particular slaves are being treated with marked brutality and possibly have been assigned to the mill as a punishment for prior resistance. Their foreheads have been tattooed with writing, which may say something like "Runaway, return to owner," as this kind of marking was mainly punitive. The shaved heads likewise mark them as slaves (cf. the episode in Petronius *Satiricon* 103 where the protagonists disguise themselves by shaving their heads and writing on them). They have shackles on their feet, which was common for slaves engaged in agricultural labor (mentioned often in Plautus where slaves constantly dread the possibility of being assigned to the mill).

fumosis tenebris vaporosae caliginis palpebras adesi "their eyelids eaten away by the smoky murkinessness of the steaming dark." As below, 9.13, a pple. (*adesi*) is followed by an acc. of respect (*palpebras*) and an instrumental abl. (*fumosis tenebris*).

adeo here probably = *ideo*, "therefore"

male luminati "badly sighted" i.e., half blind

farinulenta *hapax*. Also note that *cinis* is (atypically) f. and is apparently used figuratively to mean "dust" rather than "ash," though the deathly associations of ash are appropriate here.

9.13   Lucius now begins to describe his fellow animals, likewise beaten and abused. He begins by expressing the difficulty of adequately describing them, but the passage is full of invented vocabulary and *hapax legomena—iumentario, follicantes, tussedo, circumcursio*—indicating that for Apuleius this was a virtuoso passage, requiring the invention of new words to create an adequately descriptive narrative.

9.13.1   **iumentario contubernio** a signficant combination: Lucius at this stage admits that his comrades-in-arms or intimates are beasts of burden.

9.13.2   **capita demersi** "their heads immersed" in the feeding troughs

moles palearum The animals are wolfing down husks or chaff, which is inferior food and usually accompanied by barley or straw. Although they have mounds of it, they are also described as suffering from *scabiosa macies* below, so they are malnourished—in keeping with the general tenor of the passage.

cervices . . . follicantes; nares . . . hiulci; pectora . . . exulcerati; costas . . . renudati; ungulas . . . porrecti; corium . . . exasperati as in the section above, a string of pples. with accs. of respect and instrumental or descriptive abls.: "sagging with respect to their necks," i.e., their necks sagging, etc.

copulae sparteae tritura "by the rubbing of the rope harness"

ossium tenus "down to the bones"

perpetua castigatione The animals, like the slaves, are beaten constantly.

ungulas . . . porrecti Apparently hooves become wider when walked on excessively.

Lucius now begins to reflect on his own plight with interesting implications for our interpretation of the novel.

9.13.3 **familiae** *Familia* may refer to the whole of a household under the control of the *paterfamilias*, including relatives and domestics, but it also, as here, may refer simply to the slaves or a particular group or contingent of slaves (OLD 3).

veteris Lucii i.e., the Lucius I used to be

ultimam salutis metam "the last limit of my safety," i.e., the point beyond which Lucius cannot go and still survive

ingenita mihi curiositate Here *curiositas*, which elsewhere so often is characterized as inappropriate meddlesomeness, is more akin to an intellectual and Odyssean trait, and cheers Lucius up; knowledge, even if of sad things, is restorative.

parvi facientes *parvi* is gen. of price or value; "making little of" my presence.

9.13.4 **priscae poeticae divinus auctor** i.e., Homer, subject of *cecinit*, which introduces an indirect statement. Lucius states that Homer was right that Odysseus gained *summas virtutes* by travelling and seeing so much—just as he, Lucius, is.

summae prudentiae virum Odysseus

multarum . . . cognitu a Latin rendering of *Odyssey* 1.3. *obitu* and *cognitu* are abl. supines: "by visiting/by knowing."

civitatium i.e., *civitatum*. This gen. pl. is common, though *civitas* is not normally an *i*-stem. Varro *Lingua Latina* 8.66 cites both forms as equally correct.

gratias memini (+ dat.); a variation on *gratias agere*

asino meo . . . suo celatum tegmine The narrator, now a man, distances himself from the ass he was, and refers to it almost as if completely alien from himself.

9.13.5 **variis fortunis exercitatum** Lucius' equivalent of Odysseus' wanderings mentioned at *Odyssey* 1.1–2

etsi minus prudentem, multiscium reddidit *minus* may mean here "less (*prudens* than Odysseus)," but according to Kenney (2003) and the Groningen commentators (Hijmans et al. 1995), *minus* here means "not so, not very" rather than "less." The contrast is clearly between being wise and knowing a lot, but the precise meaning is as obscure as it is important to the interpretation of what Lucius has learned or failed to learn from being an ass. Kenney argues that Lucius, looking back at his adventures, reveals that what he has gained is sophistic polymathy, grist for his literary mill (*multiscientia*), rather than true philosophical knowledge and understanding (*prudentia*). He applies this assessment to the entire book; an older and wiser Lucius looks back on his folly.

There are other ways to read the phrase. In any case, the reference to Odysseus implies that Lucius is at least claiming an analogy between his own *curiositas* and Odysseus' thirst for knowledge of foreign lands and peoples, which gained him *summas virtutes*. We may read that comparison as ironic or not (Lucius the ass as an Odysseus is obviously comic and yet the analogy occurs in a very serious context) . If we translate "*minus*" as "less," meaning "less *prudens* than the *summae prudentiae vir*, Odysseus," Lucius is not saying that he utterly lacks *prudentia,* just less than Odysseus. Perhaps we need not read *prudentem* as quite so philosophically laden as Kenney does. One might further ask whether he means that he was *minus prudentem* as an ass (in which case, he could mean "less circumspect" or "less intelligent,") or after his initial recovery of human form, as Kenney implies. He could just be telling us that his *curiositas*, up to this point in the book, did not do all that it did for Odysseus, but did teach him many things.

Book 10

10.16.7–10.17.6 Lucius the ass at a dinner party

After being sold to various owners, most of them cruel, abusive, or
poverty-stricken, Lucius is finally bought by two cooks who treat
him well. He is discovered eating the luxurious leftovers made for
the master's dinner, and when this is brought to the master Thiasus'
attention, Lucius is invited to dine with his guests, to the amusement
of all. The guests feed him the foods most likely to be abhorrent to
an ass and laugh to see him consume them all. Zimmerman (2000)
points out the parallel with the Risus Festival in which Lucius is
most prominently the butt of laughter. This scene is the culmination
of the confusion of Lucius' humano-animal identity, since he is here
a human trapped in an animal body pretending to be human (cf. his
early experiences at 4.4 above).

10.16.7   **quod dictum** Someone had suggested that the ass might like
a glass of wine.

valde enim fieri potest ut . . . "it certainly could very well be
that . . ." Both *valde* and *enim* assert the truth of the statement
that was made in jest.

contubernalis noster i.e., Lucius

10.16.8   **puer** i.e., slave

lautum . . . cantherum mulso contempera "mingle with
honey-wine this washed (*lautum*) cup"; i.e., wash this cup
and mix in some honey-wine. Note that this large cup (*gran-
dissimum* below) is gold, indicating the wealth of Thiasus.

parasito The "parasite" is literally someone who eats at an-
other's table, a guest, but becomes a figure of ridicule in com-
edy, often a glutton who flatters his host excessively to be
rewarded with sumptuous meals. It is not clear how much
of the resonance of theatrical comedy applies here, but it is
clearly comic for an ass to be a *parasitus*.

simul quod ei praebiberim commoneto *quod* with the subjunctive is used here instead of an acc. + infinitive construction: "remind him that . . ."; *commoneto* is fut. imperative.

10.16.9 **ulla . . . ratione** "in any manner"

contorta in modum linguae postrema labia Lucius curves his lower lip into a sort of tongue. Some editors emend, but Zimmerman (2000) explains that Lucius often uses his lower lip to attempt something human, as he would use his tongue if it were not the thick tongue of an ass.

10.17.1 **emptoribus meis** in apposition to *servis suis;* i.e., the cooks who bought Lucius

quadruplum pretium Lucius was purchased for eleven *denarii* at 10.13 and now will be sold for four times that, still probably a low price. The references to his price bring to mind the slavery motif.

liberto suo The freedman is wealthy in his own right, but apparently a client of Thiasus.

magnam praefatus diligentiam "first making a request for great care (in handling me)"

10.17.2 **quo se . . . commendatiorem faceret** *quo* + compar. in a rel. clause of purpose (A&G 531 2a)

voluptates eius instruebat Note that *eius* refers to the master; the freedman was providing pleasure for him via Lucius' tricks.

10.17.3 **(ad) mensam accumbere suffixo cubito** referring to the Roman way of dining: reclining at table while leaning on one elbow

10.17.4 **quodque** "and the thing which . . . "

verbis nutum commodare "match gestures to words," (Zimmerman). The idea seems to be that Lucius will substitute a gesture for words, rather than that he will respond to words with a gesture. He is engaging in proto-human communication.

quod nollem relato, quod vellem deiecto capite Lucius is to signify what he does *not* want by raising his head and what he *does* want by lowering it, the usual gestures of refusal and assent in ancient Greece and Rome.

alterna conivens i.e., blinking alternately

sitiensque circumstantial pple.: "when thirsty"

10.17.5 **facerem** potential subjunctive

humano ritu ederem pleraque The idea is that Lucius is at risk of doing too many things in a human manner and that he could be considered a bad omen.

rati "having considered" (or, for smoothness of translation, "considering"). The implied subject is simply "people" or his trainers.

me obtruncatum vulturiis opimum pabulum redderent i.e., "after cutting me up, they would offer me . . ." cf. the sad fate of the *doppelganger* ass at 4.4–5, as well as the fate Lucius imagines for himself there: being left by the robbers to be prey for wolves and birds.

10.17.6 **rumor . . . quo** "a rumor by which" Lucius made his master famous

sodalem convivamque The brotherhood between Thiasus and Lucius, man and ass, is remarkable, yet, as Zimmerman points out, Thiasus later uses Lucius in a cruel and humiliating manner.

Book 11

Toward the end of Book 10, when Lucius has become famous as a performing ass, an aristocratic matron falls in love with him and meets with him secretly to make love. When the groom in charge of Lucius reveals this to his master, Thiasus plans to exhibit Lucius in the arena copulating with a human woman, but, for reasons of propriety, it must be a condemned woman who will later be eaten by wild beasts. Lucius is ashamed to mate publicly with this woman who is a multiple muderess (we hear her gruesome story at 10.23–28) and is also afraid of being devoured by the beasts who will be sent out to punish her, so he manages to escape and arrives at the shore at Cenchreae (near Corinth) and falls asleep on the beach. He awakes in awe of the full moon.

Fig. 4 Isis with urn and sistrum, second century CE. Capitoline Museum, Rome. Wikimedia Commons.

11.1–2 Lucius' prayer

11.1.1–11.2.4 **Circa . . . periculorum** all one very long sentence strung together with pples., adjs., abl. absolutes and conjs.

11.1.1 **primam . . . noctis vigiliam** See above on 3.21 where the same phrase is used, immediately prior to Lucius' metamorphosis

candore nimio abl. of manner dependent on *praemicantis*

lunae completum orbem The moon is full. Critics have claimed that this full moon can be precisely dated to 166 CE, given that the festival of the Ploiaphesia (11.17) takes place on March 5. There was a full moon that night in 109, 128, and 166 CE. Such a calculation is certainly excessively literal for a fictional work—though it is fun to imagine the exact day.

11.1.2   **certus** agreeing with an understood *ego*, introduces an indi-
rect statement with infinitives, most of them passive.: *pollere,
regi, vegetari, augeri, imminui*

summatem deam Lucius feels the presence of a goddess man-
ifest in the moon—a supreme goddess. He does not yet know
who she is, and later she appears embodied in a female shape.
There is nothing contradictory about the multiformity of this
goddess, as several Graeco-Roman goddesses are associated
with the moon, and their powers are cosmic/astronomical
as well as more traditionally anthropomorphic. Yet, there is
nothing quite like this prayer to the moon-goddess in ancient
literature.

prorsus with *regi*

providentia Lucius understands that Isis is watching over
and has power over all beings, animate and inanimate. At
11.15, the *providentia* of Isis is contrasted with the blindness
of *Fortuna*, activating the sense of "seeing" in *providentia*.
The world that has hitherto seemed to be ruled by random
forces is now revealed to be in the control of a rational orga-
nizing force. *Providentia* is an important concept in Middle
Platonist thought, often used as a counterbalance to the tyr-
anny of Fate in Stoic thought. Middle Platonists believe that
freedom of will exists along with divine Providence, while
Stoics are strongly deterministic. Providence, for Middle Pla-
tonists, is superior to Fate, though it still involves the con-
trol and guidance of the universe by a supreme being (Dillon
1996, 320–26). At *De Platone* 1.12 (205), Apuleius contrasts
providentia and *fatum*: Providence is the *divina sententia* pro-
tecting the prosperity of those it cares about, whereas Fate is a
divine law, by means of which God's inevitable thoughts and
plans are fulfilled. The distinction between Providence and
Fate in the *Metamorphoses* is contentious (see Graverini 2012
and Drews 2012). Whether or not Apuleius is consistent in
his views about Providence and Fate, both within this work
and between the philosophical works and his fiction, in this

passage, it is evident that Providence, identified with Isis, is a kindlier force helping to overcome the harshness of Fate.

pecuina et ferina n. pls. as substantives; there is a distinction between domestic animals and wild ones.

luminis numinisque nutu Note the incantatory quality of the Latin, entirely appropriate to the magical-divine context.

(lunae) incrementis consequenter augeri . . . referring to the moon's waxing and waning. Other Latin authors (especially Pliny the Elder *NH* 2.221) similarly claim that the moon's phases affect both animate and inanimate entities.

11.1.3 **fato** The construction now moves to abl. absolute: *fato . . . satiato et spem salutis . . . subministrante.* Usually Lucius speaks of Fortuna harassing him, but here Fate seems to take on that same antagonistic quality.

scilicet an important word: "presumably, evidently." Lucius merely *assumes* that fate is relenting.

licet "although"

statui the main verb governing all of 11.2–3

11.1.4 **purificandi studio** *studio* functions much as *causa* + gen. of the gerund would: "for the sake of/with enthusiasm for purifying."

septiesque . . . Pythagoras Pythagoras is, of course, the sixth century BCE philosopher/mathematician/mystic from Samos, most famous today for the Pythagorean theorem, who had extensive and complex theories about numbers. It is not clear exactly why Lucius claims that seven is *religionibus aptissimum*, but it is a cosmic number corresponding to the number of planets (seven including the sun but excluding the earth in a geocentric universe) and a harmonic number corresponding to the seven strings of the lyre (Burkert 1972, 310–11, 351, 354). Perhaps most to the point, it is associated with "opportunity" (*kairos*) and Athena as the "virginal prime number" among the first ten, which "neither begets another nor is begotten by any" (Burkert 1972, 467). At this moment, Lucius is in a state of innocence and about to embark on a new beginning or opportunity. In some texts, seven is considered a "perfect number" (Plutarch, *On Isis and Osiris* 10; Cicero, *De Re Publica* 6.12), though in most Pythagorean texts ten is the perfect number. Griffiths refers to several Egyptian sources that make it clear that to do an action seven times was frequent in Egyptian magical practice (112). Pythagoras may also be introduced for other reasons, such as his importance to Middle Platonists, his connection with flux and change as seen in Ovid *Metamorphoses* Book 15, his association with Egypt, or his belief in the transmigration of souls between humans and animals.

laetus et alacer Because Lucius is crying (*lacrimoso vultu*), many editors either omit these words altogether or transpose them so that the passage above says *laetus et alacer exurgo* and this passage merely has *alacer*. Yet clearly Lucius' tears express joy, relief, and religious awe, and they are not incompatible with happiness.

11.2.1 **"Regina caeli"** Lucius appears to be speaking aloud here (and crying) while still in the form of a donkey, though at 3.25 he says he is *voce privatus*. (Ancient prayer was almost always delivered aloud, and the words following his speech describe him as pouring forth his prayer and making wretched lamentations: *fusis precibus/ adstructis miseris lamentationibus*.) The presence of Isis has miraculously given him a voice just as she gives Aesop a voice in the *Anonymous Life of Aesop*. His prayer is beautifully structured, one long sentence for most of 11.2, with prayerful and incantatory repetition; after speculating on which of four female deities appears before him, Ceres, Venus, Diana, or Proserpina, (*sive, seu, seu, seu*) and adding complimentary descriptions of their powers and achievements, a familiar structure in ancient prayers to an unknown deity, he forcefully asks for release (*tu ... tu ... tu ... sit ... sit*). Lucius is aware only that the deity must be female, and there does not appear to be any clear reason why he chooses these four. Isis later introduces further goddesses by whose names she is often called. See Introduction for discussion of Isis and "henotheism."

Ceres Lucius here refers rather obliquely to the myth of the abduction of Proserpina (Persephone) by Hades. In this version, Ceres (Demeter) introduces agriculture after recovering her daughter and dwells in Eleusis (outside Athens) where the Greeks celebrated her mysteries.

vetustae glandis ferino remoto pabulo *vetustae glandis* is gen. of material ("food consisting of the ancient acorn"); *ferino remoto pabulo*: abl. absolute. Latin literature portrays primitive man eating acorns (e.g., Lucretius 5.939). Note also the characterization of Isis as a divinity who humanizes us and separates us from bestial existence, in the context of Lucius' prayers to be freed of his animal form.

miti domesticated food, cultivated grain

caelestis Venus with reference to her manifestation as the moon. In his other works, Apuleius opposes heavenly or *caelestis* Venus with Venus *vulgaris*, the carnal and lust-ridden Venus (*Apology* 12, modelled on Pausanias' speech in Plato's *Symposium*). Yet it is interesting (ironic?) here that *caelestis Venus* is immediately credited with having invented sex. Also, *caelestis* is perhaps a nod toward the North African goddess Caelestis, a Romanized form of the Punic Tanit, who had associations with both the moon and Aphrodite.

sexuum diversitatem . . . sociasti "you united the diversity of the sexes," i.e., you brought together the two different sexes, male and female.

aeterna subole humano genere propagato The idea is not that Venus necessarily created the human race, but that through continual reproduction she kept the race going.

Paphi Paphos is on Cyprus, considered Venus' birthplace and site of an important sanctuary.

sacrario abl. of location without a prep.; poetic

11.2.2   **Phoebi soror** sister of Apollo, i.e., Diana (Artemis)

partu fetarum medelis lenientibus recreato *fetarum* refers
to female animals that have recently given birth; *partu rec-
reato* is abl. absolute: "the birthings of female animals being
relieved by your soothing remedies." Diana was, among other
things, a goddess of childbirth.

praeclaris delubris Ephesi locative. The temple of Artemis
at Ephesus (in Asia Minor) was one of the Seven Wonders of
the World. The cult image of Artemis/Diana there featured
a chest of multiple breasts (though some say they are bulls'
testicles) and clearly connected this goddess with fertility and
the nurturing of the young.

veneraris pass. in meaning, though *veneror* is a deponent verb
(archaic and late Latin)

nocturnis ululatibus abl. of description

horrenda Proserpina triformi facie Proserpina, queen of the
Underworld, is *horrenda* because to see her is to experience
death, even though she is portrayed here as a kindly protec-
tor who keeps ghosts underground. She is here assimilated
somewhat to Hecate, who is commonly "triform" and also a
chthonic yet protective deity who keeps the ghosts from es-
caping from the Underworld (*larvales impetus comprimens*).
It may seem odd that Lucius would identify the goddess of the
Underworld with the moon, but Plutarch, for example, talks
of a Persephone-Selene (*selene* = moon in Greek).

All of these goddesses are to some degree described in
terms that turn out to be Isiac; Isis is connected with fertility
of both plants and humans, the development of civilization,
and death—or control over the terrifying aspects of death and
the Underworld.

11.2.3   **ista luce feminea** Lucius has finished his survey of possible
identities for the moon goddess and now refers again to the
moon itself.

udis ignibus F says *undis*, which has been emended to *udis* by most editors. It is best to understand *ignis* here as something like "light" or "radiance" rather than "fire." The moon was considered damp by many ancient writers (e.g., Macrobius and Plutarch) in contrast with the parching effects of the (male) sun, perhaps because of the dew it seems to deposit on the ground in the morning.

solis ambagibus dispensans incerta lumina *solis* is probably from *solus, -a, -um* rather than from *sol, solis*; the moon makes its revolutions alone, rather than in company like constellations. *Incerta* refers to the variation in the moon's light depending on its phases.

quoquo nomine . . . "by whatever name" etc., summarizing his attempts to identify her and covering himself in case he has offended the goddess by missing her true name, as is common in ancient prayer

11.2.4 **saevis exanclatis casibus** abl. of separation, "relief *from* the cruel misfortunes I have endured"

sit . . . sit jussives

si (ali)quod offensum numen . . . It is interesting to note that Lucius does not have any feelings of guilt or remorse, does not perceive any fault or sin that he may have committed as a result of which he deserved this harsh transformation, though he here raises the possibility that some deity might have been offended. The priest of Isis will later offer an interpretation, but for Lucius, at least, the causation remains opaque.

After his prayer, Lucius falls asleep and sees a vision of a goddess rise from the sea. He describes her wondrous appearance, starting with her hair. She is described as looking much like the Hellenized Isis with all her Egyptian accoutrements and iconography and she speaks to Lucius. Notice (1) the extravagant claims Isis makes for herself—she claims to be the *prima caelitum*, i.e., the *first* of all divinities; (2) the monotheistic, or more properly, "henotheistic" tenor of the passage. Isis calls herself the *facies uniformis* of all the gods and goddesses and refers to her *numen unicum*; (3) her cosmic powers; while she is, for Lucius, primarily a savior goddess, she can be so because she has such broad powers.

11.5.1 and 11.5.3–4 The goddess speaks

11.5.1 **En adsum** Isis speaks in the form of an "aretalogy," detailing her powers and attributes in the first person. Many such aretalogies survive from the period, as papyri or as votive or grave inscriptions. In the Kyme aretalogy, for example, a papyrus in Greek from the first or second century CE, Isis begins saying, "I am Isis" and goes on for about fifty lines listing her powers and accomplishments (e.g., "I invented writing"). The form may be Egyptian in origin.

rerum . . . uniformis In the first several lines, Isis catalogues her attributes in a grammatically consistent way, with a noun/substantive accompanied by a gen.

rerum naturae parens, elementorum omnium domina There are echoes of the praise of Venus as prime generative principle from Lucretius' *De Rerum Natura* here (see above on 4.30)—i.e., traditional Latin literature—while at the same time the passage describes Isis in terms familiar from Egyptian cult (see Griffiths 1975 for great detail on both the Old Kingdom and Hellenistic Egyptian background).

saeculorum progenies initialis The exact meaning of the phrase is obscure, but it obviously indicates that Isis was around close to the beginning of time.

deorum dearumque facies uniformis "the single form that fuses all gods and goddesses" (Griffiths); "my one person manifests the aspects of all gods and goddesses" (Hanson). Note the way that Isis does not exclude, but rather encompasses the identity of all the other divinities.

quae . . . orbis Isis now turns to a series of rel. clauses to list her attributes.

nutibus meis Gods are frequently represented as controlling the world with a nod of the head.

multiformi specie . . . nomine multiiugo One of Isis' most prominent attributes is her multiformity; cf. Plutarch *Isis and Osiris* 53,372E.

In the brief intervening portion, Isis enumerates the different names given to her in different regions of the world: "The Athenians call me Cecropian Minerva; the Eleusinians call me Ceres, some call me Bellona, Hecate," etc. "But," says Isis, "the Ethiopians and Egyptians call me Isis."

11.5.3   **Aethiopes utrique** The text is uncertain, but if this is the correct reading, it refers to the idea that there were two groups of Ethiopians, one at the rising and one at the setting of the sun (*Odyssey* 1.22–25). Ethiopians are often regarded in Classical texts as the most distant of races and certainly as alien to Greek and Roman culture.

caeremoniis propriis . . . vero nomine Apuleius makes Isis emphasize the idea that it is the Ethiopians and Egyptians who worship her properly and know her true name. Plutarch, by contrast, states that "Isis is a Greek name" (*Isis and Osiris* 2.351f.). The foreignness of this goddess is something of a surprise after Lucius enumerated only the Graeco-Roman names of goddesses in 11.2 when speculating on the identity of the deity of the moon.

11.5.4   **adsum** Isis now emphasizes her identity as savior goddess who will help Lucius.

mitte iam fletus et lamentationes omitte, depelle maerorem Isis essentially tells Lucius three times to cheer up.

After his vision and some instructions from Isis, Lucius witnesses a prelude to the rites and then a procession of Isiac worshippers, including images of the gods, religious accoutrements, musical accompaniment, and finally the priest bearing roses.

11.13 At last!

11.13.1 **sacerdos** At 11.12, a priest in the Isiac procession had come near, bearing a wreath with roses. Earlier, at 11.6, Isis had appeared to Lucius in a dream instructing him what to do when he saw the priest in the procession, and letting him know that she was also appearing to this *sacerdos*.

oraculi An *oraculum* is here (and primarily) a divine utterance made through the agency of a priest, not what we might think of as an "oracle" such as the Delphic oracle.

mandati muneris i.e., the task required of him by Isis when she visited him in a dream

11.13.2 **micanti** abl. within the abl. absolute. In Classical usage, *-e* would be the proper ending for an abl. pple. used adjectivally, but Apuleius is flexible in his abl. endings.

coronam . . . avido ore susceptam cupidus promissi devoravi The order of words in this long sentence follows Lucius' actions, and the distance of *coronam* from *susceptam* keeps us in suspense. (*Promissi* refers to the "promise" offered in Lucius' dream, that he would be restored to human form). Some see in Lucius' eagerness and perhaps greed (*avido, cupidus*) a sign that he has not "learned" anything from his trials as an ass. On the other hand, he could just be very eager to be human again!

11.13.3-5 Lucius' "anamorphosis" echoes his metamorphosis at 3.21, with a few variations.

11.13.4 **pedum plantae per ungulas in digitos exeunt** "the soles of my feet grew out through my hooves into toes" (Hanson), an odd way to imagine the recovery of toes

manus . . . in erecta porriguntur officia "my hands were no longer feet, but stretched out for their upright functions." Another odd conceit. Both of these descriptions of Lucius' re-transformation denaturalize the human body in a work that blurs animal-human boundaries and asks us to rethink these distinctions.

11.13.5 **os et caput rutundatur** sing. verb perhaps because the mouth and head are considered jointly. The elongated head and mouth of the ass return to their rounded human shape.

quae me potissimum cruciabat "the thing which especially tortured me." Though we actually do not hear an inordinate amount about his tail, its appearance marks him as an animal inasmuch as there is no human equivalent.

Both Lucius' metamorphosis and his anamorphosis echo the anamorphosis of Io at Ovid, *Metamorphoses* 1.738–47. Io is one of the few people in Ovid's long account of metamorphoses who, like Lucius, recovers her human form (she had been a cow). She was traditionally associated with Isis from at least the fifth century BCE, perhaps because Isis is sometimes represented with cows' horns and Ovid concludes his account by saying (747) "now she is worshipped by the linen-wearing crowd," i.e., Isiacs. Thus, Apuleius' evocation of Ovid's account brings Isis into the text subliminally at an early moment (3.25).

11.13.6 **populi . . . religiosi** The distinction is between the general onlookers and the faithful for whom this transformation is a clear sign of the divine power of Isis.

consimilem nocturnis imaginibus magnificentiam The faithful admire the correspondence between the nocturnal vision and the magnificent reality, though only the priest received the nocturnal vision—probably a minor slip by Apuleius rather than anything significant.

reformationis the Latin word for "metamorphosis," which is Greek and used only in the title of the work. The faithful are astounded at how easy it is for Isis to change Lucius back.

caelo manus adtendentes lifting their hands to heaven and loudly acclaiming Isis' beneficence—in the ancient manner of prayer

11.15.1–3 The priest's analysis

In 11.14, Lucius stands dumbfounded at his good fortune and is given a cloak to hide his nakedness. The priest who had received the nocturnal vision from Isis now addresses him. This section has often been read as a key to interpreting the events of the *Metamorphoses*, offering what may seem a satisfying moral lesson: Lucius indulged in servile pleasures and ill-advised curiosity and reaped the reward. Yet, this explanation by the priest does not entirely square with the events leading up to Lucius' metamorphosis. It is surely true that he was obliquely warned about the dangers of magic in the embedded tales and ekphrases of Books 1–2, was directly warned by his aunt later on, and was, in general, prying into forbidden realms. Yet, there seems nothing reprehensible in his dalliance with Fotis (as is sometimes claimed), judging by the *mores* of the time. Further, Lucius' misadventures seem more the effect of *saeva Fortuna*, as the priest himself says, than any deliberate punishment by a divine being; on the most basic level, he was simply given the wrong potion. This speech seems *but one interpretation* of the narrative (cf. Penwill 1990); as noted above, Lucius recognizes no particular guilt, and Isis herself in her speech to him (above, 11.5–6) says nothing about punishment, only deliverance; he must henceforth serve her and she will protect him.

11.15.1   **exanclatis laboribus . . . actus procellis** The construction changes, first an abl. absolute and then a pple. in the nom. with instrumental abls.

magnisque Fortunae tempestatibus et magnis actus procellis Construe *actus* with both phrases. Note the figurative language: Lucius has been tossed about by winds and is coming into a port of safety. The sea imagery connects to the ritual of the *navigium Isidis* in the next section, 11.16.

portum Quietis et aram Misericordiae In general, what the priest of Isis offers here corresponds to Lucius' prayers at 11.2 for peace, rest, and succor, and emphasizes Isis' role as protective goddess. The two abstract concepts of quiet and pity are semi-deified, but do not appear to correspond directly to any particular deities or icons known in the worship of Isis. The metaphor of the "port of Quiet" is suitable for a ritual taking place in the port of Cenchreae, and an altar of Mercy is attested both in Athens (Pausanias 1.17.1) and Rome (Servius *ad Aen.* 8.342). Griffiths suggests that the source for Apuleius' nautical imagery here may be genuinely Egyptian, given both Isis' connections to the sea and Egyptian images of the soul on a boat (245). Mainly, though, a port and an altar are familiar images of protection.

natales . . . dignitas references to Lucius' aristocratic *prosapia* introduced at 1.1, 1.2, 2.3, and 3.15. The verb *profuit* is sing. despite having three subjects (*natales, dignitas,* and *doctrina*), agreeing with the nearest of the subjects, *doctrina.*

ipsa qua flores . . . doctrina Separate out nom. (*ipsa*) and abl. (*qua*).

doctrina Lucius mentions his education in Athens at 1.24, and Fotis refers to his *doctrina* and *ingenium* at 3.15; he will soon become a successful *advocatus* in Rome. Some have also seen a semi-autobiographical reference to Apuleius' own Platonic *doctrina.* Yet the main point to keep in mind here is the Isiac priest's insistent separation of birth, behavior, *doctrina,* and religious salvation.

lubrico virentis aetatulae *lubrico* here is the abl. of a n. substantive formed from the adj. *lubricus.* The abl. seems to be essentially locative—"*in* the slipperiness of youth."

ad serviles delapsus voluptates See above. The *voluptates* here do not refer exclusively to Lucius' erotic liaison with a slave, but indicate more generally that he indulged in pleasures that someone of high birth like him should have known to avoid.

curiositatis inprosperae curiosity again. The priest clearly condemns curiosity, but it is also curiosity that brought Lucius to this blessed state, one of the paradoxes of the book.

reportasti i.e., *reportavisti*

11.15.2   **utcumque . . . inprovida produxit malitia** *improvida malitia*
is abl. The priest emphasizes the apparent randomness and
powerlessness of blind Fortune; she tortured Lucius and raged
against him, but somehow (*utcumque*) her blindness (echoed
in *inprovida*, unforeseeing), led him to this state of blessed-
ness.

eat nunc a modified form (jussive subjunctive) of the sarcastic
phrase *i nunc*: "let her go now"

**quorum sibi vitas in servitium deae nostrae maiestas vin-
dicavit** "whose lives the majesty of our goddess has freed
into servitude to her." The paradox that Lucius is freed by his
servitude to Isis is made even more explicit at the end of the
priest's speech (not excerpted here): *nam cum coeperis deae
servire, tunc magis senties fructum tuae libertatis* ("when you
have become a slave to the goddess, then you will most feel the
fruit of your liberty").

casus infestus The phrase seems to be simply a variation on
saeva Fortuna, less personified and more abstract.

servitium Note that the priest refers to Lucius' asinine state as
one of *servitium*, reinforcing the slavery subtext.

11.15.3   **quid latrones, quid ferae . . . profuit** once again, multiple
subjects with a sing. verb. *Prosum* takes the dat. here.

ambages reciprocae "aimless wanderings"; both words ex-
press the idea of wandering back and forth.

mortis cotidianae/ nefariae Fortunae Attach the modifiers
appropriately. Fortune is represented as even more deliber-
ately hostile this time.

Fortunae, sed videntis Isis here takes on the role of "For-
tune," a role familiar in her Hellenistic manifestation where
she is called Isis-Fortuna or Isis-Tyche. This power of the
gods to overcome fate can be traced back to original Egyptian
sources (Griffiths 1975, 241–44), a power which Isis claims
elsewhere in Book 11 (11.6; 11.25). It is important that she is

here designated as "seeing Fortune" as opposed to the blind
Fortune that has hounded Lucius.

11.27.9 The man from Madauros

Lucius has now undergone initiation into the rites of Isis. A year
passes. He begins to have dreams that urge him to undergo more
initiations; he has not yet been inducted into the rites of Osiris. He
eventually learns that the priest who will initiate him into these mys-
teries is named Asinius Marcellus, and he finds that Asinius has also
had a dream.

11.27.9   **sibi visus est quiete proxima** *sibi* refers to Asinius Marcellus;
visus est is the usual language for a dream or vision; *quies* here
= sleep, i.e., night.

et de eius ore There is apparently a gap in the transmitted text
(the ellipse in the printed text represents this gap, not an edi-
torial omission). *Eius* here refers to Osiris, from whose mouth
each mortal's fate is told.

quo singulorum fata dictat (*ore* is the antecedent of *quo*.)
Osiris is represented, like Isis above, as having authority over
fate and determining the course of human lives.

dum magno deo coronas exaptat The garlands are presum-
ably for a statue of the god.

audisse (= *audivisse*) infinitive in indirect statement, but the
exact verb on which it depends seems to be lost. The subject of
audisse is the *sacerdos*.

Madaurensem The priest has had a dream that a man from
Madauros is being sent to him for initiation. Madauros was a
town in Africa Proconsularis, now M'Daourouch in Algeria,
the hometown of Apuleius, not Lucius. The substitution is in-
triguing and various suggestions have been offered to cope
with it, e.g., (1) emend to *Corinthiensem* on the grounds that
either Apuleius slipped or an early scribe who confused Lu-
cius and Apuleius had changed it to *Madaurensem*; (2) assume

that the priest's information is wrong, that this is another in-
stance of misreading in a narrative full of different interpreta-
tions; (3) think of this as a *sphragis* or a kind of stamp signing
the work as Apuleius' here at the end of the novel; (4) read this
as a sign that the whole work has been autobiographical, on a
highly metaphorical level. In any case, it is a reminder of the
North African origins of the text, an intrusion of a different
cultural landscape. One might combine the last two possibili-
ties and read the whole novel as a personal saga of the immi-
grant.

illi . . . ipsi The first refers to Lucius/Apuleius and the second
to the priest, dats. of agent (possibly dats. of reference) after
comparari.

comparari The clause is still within indirect discourse after
audisse, so construe: *illi gloriam . . . comparari*, "glory would
be acquired by him." We expect a fut. infinitive, as the events
have not yet occurred, and occasionally a pres. infinitive can
express fut. time in indirect discourse (A&G 584b), but per-
haps this should be translated with the pres.

grande compendium The priest will receive great monetary
rewards. This is not what we expect from the spiritual life
and, along with other passages in Book 11, has led a number
of critics to question the motives of the Isiac priests and there-
fore the meaning of the whole conversion experience. See In-
troduction, "Other readings."

11.30.3–5 The end: Lucius is made a "pastophor"

11.30.3   Lucius has undergone one further initiation, but is visited
again by the gods and urged to undergo a third initiation, as-
sured by the priests that he is blessed to be called repeatedly.
He abstains from meat and ritually prepares in other ways for
this final revelation.

11.30.3   **deus deum magnorum potior** (*deum = deorum*); the phrase
clearly means "greatest of the gods," but it is not clear whether

the compar. *potior* here is constructed with a gen. of comparison in the Greek manner (i.e., "god greater than the great gods") or whether the compar. has superl. force. Griffiths 1975 (341) compares the Semitic and Egyptian idiom "god of gods and king of kings," a construction Apuleius could have known through Hellenized Isiac texts, so the phrase could be translated "very powerful god of the great gods," meaning "god of gods," i.e., "greatest of the gods."

maiorum summus . . . maximorum regnator The excessive number of superls. assures us that Osiris is absolutely the highest of the high—and that we are reaching the end of Lucius' saga.

sed coram . . . visus est "he appeared to me in my sleep, having deigned (*dignatus*) to welcome me (*me recipere*) face to face (*coram*) with his own venerable utterance (*suo illo venerando adfamine*)."

11.30.4 **quam nunc, incunctanter . . . redderem . . . nec extimescerem** *quam* is usually emended to *quae,* but Fredouille defends the reading of F by suggesting that *tam* is elided: (*tam*)*quam nunc*: "as now." These words now express what Osiris said to Lucius in his *adfamine*, the subjunctives rendering the indirect command: "that I should unhesitatingly, as now continue as an advocate . . . "

gloriosa redderem patrocinia The phrase *patrocinia reddere* is modelled on the familiar expressions, *ius reddere* and *iudicium reddere* ("render judgment") but is hard to render literally in English: "win fame in the courts as an advocate" (Hanson). Lucius has become a successful advocate in the courts at Rome. This is not incompatible with his religious life. While he is devoted to the goddess, and later the gods, and while his devotion is remarkably focused for a pagan, he has not entered an exclusive religious life. Being a *patronus* and defending one's clients was the standard path for aristocratic Roman males, so there is nothing particularly surprising about Lucius becoming a lawyer.

malevolorum disseminationes It is interesting that Lucius' success has aroused ill-will, a brief mention that is never elaborated. Is it just the envy that inevitably accompanies success? Does it have anything to do with Lucius being an immigrant whose first language is not Latin but who nonetheless excels in the law-court? Is there anything autobiographical here, referring to his actual rivals in oratory?

ac ne . . . deservirem purpose clause. *Deservio* takes the dat., *sacris suis*, i.e., "his mysteries."

gregi cetero permixtus Lucius is a privileged initiate and wants to be separate from the ordinary worshippers.

collegium pastophorum . . . decurionum quinquennales What exactly was a *pastophor*? Evidence external to the *Metamorphoses* indicates that this was probably a relatively low-level religious office, "on the border between temple servants and the higher-ranking priests" (Egelhaaf-Gaiser 2012, 50). Some critics have therefore seen satiric implications in Lucius' inordinate pride in achieving this office. However, as Egelhaaf-Gaiser points out, within our text the office appears to be exalted and gives Lucius important access to exclusive Isiac ritual and knowledge. At 11.17, a *sacerdos maximus* calls together the *pastophori* and reads from a sacred text; Asinius Marcellus at 11.27 is designated as a *pastophorus*, and seems to have important duties, as he is to administer Lucius' second initiation. Lucius is not only a *pastophor*, but one of the *decurionum quinquennales* or "quinquennial officers," a more exalted branch of the pastophors.

11.30.5 **quaqua raso capillo** The text is in doubt, but since Lucius had ritually shaved his head before, this makes sense. *quaqua* here means "on all sides, everywhere, completely." Isiac priests shaved their heads as a matter of ritual purity.

sub illis Sullae temporibus Lucius Cornelius Sulla 138–78 BCE, consul 88, 80; dictator 82–81, mentioned here to date the introduction of these cults to Rome, yet the dating is a bit problematic; see Takacs 1995, 56–70. The cults were suppressed after the time of Sulla and not officially sanctioned until much later, though there is certainly evidence of worship from a much earlier period.

collegii . . . obibam Take in this order for the purposes of translation: *gaudens obibam munia collegii vetustissimi* [*et*] *sub illis Sullae temporibus conditi, non obumbrato vel obtecto calvitio.* It is important, however, that the final two words of the book are *gaudens obibam,* (I was performing joyously) and encapsulate the feeling of joy that pervades Book 11. Now that he is a devout follower of Egyptian cult, Lucius parades around Rome displaying his "baldness" openly. Some see him here as a figure of ridicule, bald like a clown, another bald figure commonly seen about Rome. Egelhaaf-Gaiser (2012, 47–49), however, calls attention to a set of portrait heads probably of the Flavian period that represent men with shaved heads and cultic scarring—apparently indicating that members of the elite belonging to religious cults were very comfortable publicly presenting their association with foreign religion. Others take his proud baldness as a fitting spiritual renunciation of physical appearance, especially considering Lucius' obsessive interest in hair at 2.8–9. The fact that the last word is in the impf. tense has caused some to see the story as unfinished; perhaps Lucius the narrator, now older and wiser, is looking back at his adventures and disapproving of his foolish behavior at the time. Others point out that *obeo* is frequently used in the impf. tense without a strong imperfective meaning. The word also can mean "to die," a meaning not operative here (though some have argued so) but appropriate as a closural gesture. In any case, we leave Lucius happily installed as an initiate in the cults of Isis and Osiris. Unlike the heroes and heroines of the Greek ideal novel, Lucius has not simply returned to the point where he began, but has gone through various radical changes.

Appendix

∽ *Map: Significant Locations in Apuleius' Life and the METAMORPHOSES*

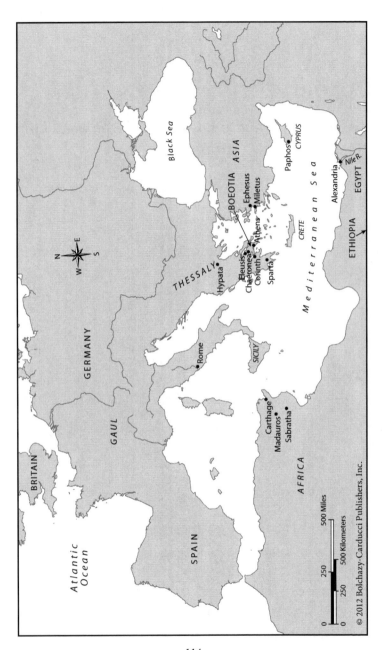

Complete Vocabulary

ā *or* **ab,** *prep.* + *abl.*, from, away from; by (*agent*)

abiciō, -ere, -iēcī, -iectum, to cast aside, throw down, take off

abigō, -ere, abēgī, abactum, to drive away

abripiō, -ere, -ripuī, -reptum, to remove

abscondō, -ere, -ī (-idī), -itum, to hide, bury

absens, *gen.* **-ntis,** *adj.*, absent

absentia, -ae *f.*, absence

absum, abesse, āfuī, —, to be absent, keep clear or refrain from

absurdē, *adv.*, preposterously, ridiculously

ac. *See* **atque**

accēdō, -ere, -cessī, -cessum, to approach

acceptus, -a, -um, *adj.*, well-liked, pleasing

accipiō, -ere, -cēpī, -ceptum, to receive, hear

accumbō, -ere, -cubuī, -cubitum, to lie down, recline at table

accurrō, -ere, -currī *or* **-cucurrī, -cursum,** to run or hurry to

aciēs, -ēī, *f.*, sharp edge, point

actor, -ōris, *m.*, performer, doer, agent

acūmen, -inis, *n.*, sharp point

ad, *prep.* + *acc.*, to, toward, at, in, for

addō, -ere, addidī, additum, to add

adedō, -ere, adēdī, adēsum, to eat away, erode

adeō, *adv.*, to such a degree, therefore (= **ideō**); **non adeō,** not so

adfāmen, -inis, *n.*, greeting, salutation (first in Apuleius)

adfectiō, -ōnis, *f.*, affection, love

adfirmō (1), to support, restore, strengthen

adfricō, -āre, -uī, adfrictum, to rub, smear on

adipiscor, -ī, adeptus sum, to gain, attain

aditus, -ūs, *m.*, entrance

adlegō, -ere, -lēgī, -lectum, to elect, admit, recruit

adluctor, -ārī, -ātus sum, to wrestle

admīrātiō, -ōnis, *f.*, admiration, wonder, astonishment

admodum, *adv.*, rather, quite

admoveō, -ēre, -mōvī, -mōtum, to move toward, bring to

adōrātiō, -ōnis, *f.*, act of worship or prayer

adōrō (1), to pray to, worship

adpetō, -ere, -īvī *or* **-iī, -ītum,** to seek, desire, attack, have an appetite for

adplaudō, -ere, -plausī, -plausum, to clap the hands, applaud

adpōnō, -ere, -posuī, -positum, to place near, set out (especially of food or drink)

adprecor, -ārī, -ātus sum, to address prayers to, invoke, beseech

adprīmē, *adv.*, extremely, very

adripiō, -ere, -ripuī, -reptum, to take hold of, seize

adsevērō (1), to declare, affirm

adsiduē, *adv.*, continually

adsiduus, -a, -um, *adj.*, consistent, persistent

adsistō, -ere, astitī, —, to stand by, attend

adsum, -esse, -fuī, —, to be present, be there

adtendō, -ere, -tendī, -tentum, to stretch out, extend

adtrahō, -ere, -traxī, -tractum, to drag toward, compel to come

aduncus, -a, -um, *adj.*, curved, hooked

adūrō, -ere, -ussī, -ustum, to scorch, burn

adusque, *prep.* + *acc.*, all the way up to

advena, -ae, *m.*, visitor, immigrant, stranger (+ gen.)

aedēs, -is, *f.* dwelling, house (in *pl.*)

Aegyptius, -a, -um, *adj.*, Egyptian

aerumna, -ae, *f.*, labor, distress

aerumnābilis, -e, *adj.*, causing misery, distressing

aes, aeris, *n.*, bronze

aestus, -ūs, *m.*, heat, anxiety

aetātula, -ae, *f.*, youth, tender age

aeternus, -a, -um, *adj.*, eternal, everlasting, unceasing

Aethiops, *gen.* **-pis,** *adj.*, Ethiopian

affātus, -ūs, *m.*, speech, conversation

afficiō, -ere, -fēcī, -fectum, to make

afflō (1), to blow on, blast, touch

affluens, *gen.* **-ntis,** *adj.*, abundant, plentiful

aggredior, -ī, -gressus sum, to approach, attack, undertake

agnitiō, -ōnis, *f.*, recognition

agō, -ere, ēgī, actum, to drive, do; **age,** come!

āiō, —, —, —, to say, affirm

āla, -ae, *f.*, wing

alacer, -cris, -cre, *adj.*, lively, quick, eager

aliēnus, -a, -um, *adj.*, different, other

aliōquīn, *adv.*, in other respects, as a general rule, anyhow

aliquantus, -a, -um, *adj.*, a certain quantity of

aliquī, -qua, -quod, *adj.*, some

aliquis, -qua, -quid, *pron.*, someone, something

alius, -a, -ud, *adj.*, different, other; **aliī . . . aliī,** some . . . others

almus, -a, -um, *adj.*, nurturing, fostering; (*alma* as substantive) nourisher, mother

alternus, -a, -um, *adj.*, alternating, alternate

altiusculē, *adv.*, rather high (only in Apuleius)

altus, -a, -um, *adj.*, high, lofty, exalted, proud

amanter, *adv.*, lovingly, amorously

amātor, -ōris, *m.*, lover

ambacu† (meaning unknown, having to do with food)

ambāgēs, -um, *f. pl.*, a roundabout or circuitous path, meanderings, wanderings to and fro

ambiō, -īre, -īvī *or* **-iī, -ītum,** to go around, surround

ambrosia, -ae, *f.*, food of the gods, a divine unguent

āmens, *gen.* **-ntis,** *adj.*, out of one's mind, demented, frantic

āmentia, -ae, *f.*, madness, frenzy

amfractus, -ūs, *m.*, winding course, detour

amiciō, -īre, amicuī *or* **amixī, amictum,** to clothe, dress

amnicus, -a, -um, *adj.*, connected with a river

amoenus, -a, -um, *adj.*, pleasing, beautiful

amor, -ōris, *m.*, love, beloved

Amor, -ōris, *m.*, Love, Cupid

amplector, -ī, -plexus sum, to embrace, take hold of, seize eagerly

amplus, -a, -um, *adj.*, large, great

amputō (1), to cut off

an, *particle*, can it really be that?, whether, or

angiportum, -ī, *n.*, a narrow passage, alley

angor, -ōris, *m.*, mental distress, anguish

animadvertō, -ere, -vertī, -versum, to notice

animal, -ālis, *n.*, animal, beast

animus, -ī, *m.*, the mind, heart, courage, passions

annus, -ī, *m.*, year

annuus, -a, -um, *adj.*, annual, yearly

ante, *prep.* + *acc.*, before, in front of

ante, *adv.*, before (in time)

antecapiō, -ere, -cēpī, -captum, to anticipate (a plan)

antependulus, -a, -um, *adj.*, hanging down in front (only in Apuleius)

ānulātus, -a, -um, *adj.*, ringed, fettered

anus, -ūs, *f.*, old woman

anxius, -a, -um, *adj.*, worried, uneasy

Apollō, -inis, *m.*, Apollo

apparō (1), to prepare

appellō (1), to call upon, address

aptus, -a, -um, *adj.*, appropriate, fitting

apud, *prep. + acc.*, among

aqua, -ae, *f.*, water

āra, -ae, *f.*, altar

arbitror, -ārī, -ātus sum, to observe, witness

arbor, -oris, *m.*, tree

arcula, -ae, *f.*, small chest, box

arcus, -ūs, *m.*, bow

ardor, -ōris, *m.*, burning, desire

argūtia, -ae, *f.*, sharpness, cleverness, wit

argūtulus, -a, -um, *adj.*, clever, shrewd

ariolor *or* **hariolor, -ārī, -ātus sum,** prophesy, divine

Aristomenēs, -is, *m.*, Aristomenes

arma, -ōrum, *n. pl.*, arms, weapons

arripiō, -ere, arripuī, arreptum, to seize, pick up

ars, artis, *m.*, art, skill

articulus, -ī, *m.*, a joint, finger

asinārius, -ī, *m.*, donkey-driver, ass-driver

asinus, -ī, *m.*, donkey, ass

aspectus, -ūs, *m.*, sight, gaze

asper, -era, -erum, *adj.*, rough, harsh, rugged

aspiciō, -ere, aspexī, aspectum, to notice, see

astus, -ūs, *m.*, cunning, trick

at, *conj.*, but

āter, ātra, ātrum, *adj.*, black, dark

atque, *conj.*, and, and also, and in fact, and indeed

Atticus, -a, -um, *adj.*, Attic, Athenian

attiguus, -a, -um, *adj.*, neighboring

Attis, -idis, *adj.*, Attic, Athenian

attonitus, -a, -um, *adj.*, stunned, awestruck, overwhelmed

auctor, -ōris, *m.*, originator, source, author

auctus, -ūs, *m.*, growth

audācia, -ae, *f.*, boldness

audax, *gen.* **-ācis,** *adj.*, daring, bold

audiō, -īre, -īvī, -ītum, to hear

auferō, auferre, abstulī, ablātum, to carry away, remove, put aside

augeō, -ēre, auxī, auctum, to increase

augustus, -a, -um, *adj.*, venerable

aureus, -a, -um, *adj.*, golden

auris, -is, *f.*, ear

Aurōra, -ae, *f.*, Aurora, goddess of the dawn

avidē, *adv.*, greedily, eagerly

avidus, -a, -um, *adj.*, greedy,
eager, ardently desirous of
avis, -is, *f.*, bird
āvolō (1), to fly away

balsamum, -ī, *n.*, balsam, an
aromatic resinous product
used as an unguent
barathrum, -ī, *n.*, chasm, pit
bāsiō (1), to kiss
beātitūdō, -inis, *f.*, blessedness
beātus, -a, -um, *adj.*, happy,
fortunate, blessed
bellus, -a, -um, *adj.*, pretty,
excellent
bene, *adv.*, well
beneficium, -ī, *n.*, kindness,
favor
benivolus, -a, -um, *adj.*, kind
bestia, -ae, *f.*, beast
bibō, -ere, -ī, —, to drink
blandē, *adv.*, charmingly,
seductively
bonus, -a, -um, *adj.*, good
bōs, bovis, *m./f.*, ox, bull
brāchium, -iī, *n.*, forearm,
arm
būbō, -ōnis, *m./f.*, the horned
owl

cadāver, -eris, *n.*, dead body,
corpse
caecitās, -ātis, *f.*, blindness
caedēs, -is, *f.*, killing,
slaughter
caedō, -ere, cecīdī, caesum,
to strike down, kill
caeles, *gen.* **-itis,** *adj.*, celestial;
(*as substantive*) divinity

caelestis, -e, *adj.*, heavenly,
divine
caelum, -ī, *n.*, sky, heavens
caerimōnia, -ae, *f.*, reverence;
(*pl.*) religious rites,
ceremonies
caerulus, -a, -um, *adj.*, blue,
blue-green
caesariēs, -ēī, *f.*, long, flowing,
or luxurious hair
calamus, -ī, *m.*, reed, pen
cālīgō, -inis, *f.*, darkness,
murkiness of thick smoke
calix, -icis, *m.*, drinking cup
calvitium, -iī, *n.*, baldness,
absence of hair
calx, -cis, *f.*, the heel, a kick
candicō, -āre, —, —, to have a
white appearance
candidātus, -a, -um, *adj.*,
whitened
candidus, -a, -um, *adj.*, bright,
white, radiant
candor, -ōris, *m.*, radiance
canīnus, -a, -um, *adj.*, relating
to a dog
canis, -is, *m./f.*, dog
canō, -ere, cecinī, cantum, to
sing
canōrus, -a, -um, *adj.*,
melodious
cantāmen, -inis, *n.*, spell,
incantation
cantharus, -ī, *m.*, large
drinking vessel with
handles
canthērius, -(i)ī, *m.*, a horse of
poor quality, nag
cantō (1), to sing

capillus, -ī, *m.*, hair of the head

capiō, -ere, cēpī, captum, to seize, catch, overcome

caput, -itis, *n.*, head

cariōsus, -a, -um, *adj.*, decayed, rotten

carmen, -inis, *n.*, song, spell

carnifex, -icis, *m.*, executioner

cārus, -a, -um, *adj.*, dear, beloved

castīgātiō, -ōnis, *f.*, beating

cāsus, -ūs, *m.*, fall, chance, situation, misfortune

catēna, -ae, *f.*, chain; (*pl.*) fetters

cauda, -ae, *f.*, tail

causa, -ae, *f.*, cause, (in abl.) for the sake of

causārius, -a, -um, *adj.*, (with **missiō**) a discharge on health grounds

cautē, *adv.*, carefully

cautēla, -ae, *f.*, a caution, warning (rare and post-classical)

cavea, -ae, *f.*, the auditorium of a theater

celebritās, -ātis, *f.*, a crowding

celebrō (1), to throng, honor, praise, celebrate

celeritās, -ātis, *f.*, speed, quickness

celerō, -āre, -āvī, —, to hasten, go quickly

cēlō (1), to hide, conceal

cēna, -ae, *f.*, dinner

centunculus, -ī, *m.*, cloth made of patchwork

Cerēs, -eris, *f.*, Ceres, goddess of grain and fruits

certē, *adv.*, certainly, surely

certō, *adv.*, certainly, without a doubt, (compar. *certius*)

certus, -a, -um, *adj.*, fixed, determined

cervix, -īcis, *f.*, neck

cēterus, -a, -um, *adj.*, (*pl.*) the rest

Chaldaeus, -a, -um, *adj.*, of the Chaldaeans, a people of southern Syria known for soothsaying

chorus, -ī, *m.*, a dance with singing accompaniment, a choral song

cibāria, -ōrum, *n. pl.*, a ration of food, food supplied to animals

cibārius, -a, -um, *adj.*, concerned with food, concerned with plain, common food

cibus, -ī, *m.*, food

cicātrix, -īcis, *f.*, wound, scar

cilium, -iī, *n.*, the upper eyelid

cinis, -eris, *m.*, ash, dust

circā, *prep. + acc.*, around

circulus, -ī, *m.*, circle

circumcursiō, -ōnis, *f.*, a running about or around, revolution (hapax)

circumeō, -īre, -īvī *or* **-iī, -itum,** to go around, make a circuit

circumferō, -ferre, -tulī, -lātum, to carry around

circumfluō, -ere, -fluxī, —, to flow around, crowd around

circumfluus, -a, -um, *adj.*,
   flowed around, surrounded
circumfundō, -ere, -fūdī,
   -fūsum, to pour; (pass.) be
   situated around
cithara, -ae, *f.*, lyre
cīvis, -is, *m./f.*, citizen
cīvitās, -ātis, *f.* a city; the
   citizens of a city
clādēs, -is, *f.*, calamity, disaster
clāmō (1), to shout
clāmor, -ōris, *m.*, a shout, noise
clārescō, -ere, clāruī, —, to be
   illuminated, become clear
clārus, -a, -um, *adj.*, loud, clear
claudus, -a, -um, *adj.*, lame,
   limping
claustrum, -ī, *n.*, gate, barrier
clēmens, *gen.* -entis, *adj.*, gentle
clīvulus, -ī, *m.*, a short slope
   (hapax)
Cnidos, -ī (Greek forms), *f.*,
   Cnidos, a town in southwest
   Caria, in Asia Minor
coetus, -ūs, *m.*, gathering,
   company, society
cōgitātus, -ūs, *m.*, thought,
   plan, scheme
cōgitō (1), to think, plan,
   decide, consider
cognitus, -ūs, *m.*, the act of
   getting to know
cognoscō, -ere, -nōvī, -nitum,
   to get to know, learn,
   investigate
cōgō, -ere, coēgi, coāctum, to
   drive together, compress
cohibeō, -ēre, -uī, -itum, to
   restrain, reduce in size

collēgium, -iī, *n.*, a college or
   board of priests
collocō (1), to put, set, place
colluviēs, -ēi, *f.*, muck, decayed
   matter, filth
colō, -ere, coluī, cultum, to
   dwell, worship
columna, -ae, *f.*, column
comes, -itis, *m./f.*, companion
cōmiter, *adv.*, courteously,
   pleasantly
comitor, -ārī, -ātus sum, to
   accompany
commendātus, -a, -um, *adj.*,
   acceptable, agreeable
commentum, -ī, *n.*, invention,
   device
commeō, -āre, -āvī, -ātum, to
   come and go, go back and
   forth, travel
commīlitō, -ōnis, *m.*, a fellow
   soldier
comminus, *adv.*, at close
   quarters, hand-to-hand (of
   fighting)
commodō (1), to provide
commodum, *adv.*, at this very
   moment, just
commonefaciō, -ere, -fēcī,
   -factum, remind (+ gen. of
   thing)
commoneō, -ēre, -uī, -itum, to
   remind
commonstrō (1), to point out,
   reveal
commoveō, -ēre, -mōvī,
   -mōtum, to move, stir
commūnis, -e, *adj.*, shared,
   common

comparō (1), to prepare, devise, acquire

compellō, -ere, -pulī, -pulsum, to force

compendium, -iī, *n.*, gain, profit

compleō, -ēre, -ēvī, -ētum, to fill, complete

complicō, -āre, -āvī *or* **-uī, -itum,** to fold, bend

compressiō, -ōnis, *f.*, squeezing, compression

comprimō, -ere, -pressī, -pressum, to squeeze, press, hold back, curb

comprobō (1), to approve, ratify

cōnātus, -ūs, *m.*, effort

concēdō, -ere, -cessī, -cessum, to go away, withdraw

concīdō, -ere, -cīdī, -cīsum, to cut up, chop

concinnō (1), to prepare, arrange, construct, concoct

concitus, -a, -um, *adj.*, headlong

conclūdō, -ere, -clūsī, -clūsum, to shut

condiō, -īre, -īvī *or* **-iī, -ītum,** to flavor food, season

condō, -ere, -didī, -itum, to establish, store up, found

cōnectō, -ere, -nexuī, -nexum, to join, fasten, link

conferō, -ferre, contulī, collatum, to bring together; **capita conferre,** to bring heads together in conference

confestim, *adv.*, immediately

conficiō, -ere, -fēcī, -fectum, to finish, traverse

confluō, -ere, -fluxī, —, to flow together, flock together

congredior, -ī, -gressus sum, to approach, contend, fight

congregō (1), to bring together, assemble

congruentia, -ae, *f.*, accordance, consistency

coniunx, -ugis, *m./f.*, spouse

cōnīveō, -ēre, conīvī *or* **conīxī, —,** to close the eyes

conlābor, -ī, -lapsus sum, to slip or sink, collapse

conloquor, -ī, -locūtus sum, to talk with, converse with, speak to

conlustrō (1), to look over, explore

conplector, -ī, -plexus sum, to embrace, surround, encircle

consecō, -āre, secuī, -sectum, to cut into pieces, cut up

consentiō, -īre, -sensī, -sensum, to agree, conspire

conseptum, -ī, *n.*, an enclosure

consequenter, *adv.*, (+ dat.) in accordance with

conserō, -ere, -seruī, -sertum, to entwine, join together

consīderō (1), to observe, contemplate

consilium, -iī, *n.*, deliberation, scheme

consimilis, -e, *adj.*, similar

consonus, -a, -um, *adj.*, harmonious, singing in unison conspectus, -ūs, *m.*, sight

conspectus, -a, -um, *adj.*, visible, attracting attention, conspicuous

conspiciō, -ere, -spexī, -spectum, to catch sight of, see

conspicuus, -a, -um, *adj.*, clearly seen, visible, remarkable

contegō, -ere, -texī, -tectum, to cover, clothe

contemperō (1), to temper a drink (hapax)

contentus, -a, -um, *adj.*, content, satisfied

conterreō, -ēre, -terruī, -territum, to frighten thoroughly

contingō, -ere, -tigī, -tactum, to touch

continuus, -a, -um, *adj.*, continual, unremitting

contorqueō, -ēre, -torsī, -tortum, to twist around

contrārius, -a, -um, *adj.*, opposite

contruncō (1), to gobble up

contubernālis, -is, *m./f.*, tent-mate (military), intimate friend

contubernium, -iī, *n.*, an association, band, or brotherhood

contumēlia, -ae, *f.*, indignity, insult

conveniō, -īre, -vēnī, -ventum, to come together; **in manum convenīre,** to come into the charge of her husband

conversor, -ārī, -versātus sum, to associate with

convertō, -ere, -vertī, -versum, to change, transform

convīva, -ae, *m./f.*, table companion, guest

cooperiō, -īre, -operuī, -opertum, to cover up

cōperculum, -ī, *n.*, lid

cōpiōsus, -a, -um, *adj.*, rich, plentiful

cōpula, -ae, *f.*, leash, harness

coquō, -ere, coxī, coctum, to cook

cor, cordis, *m.*, heart

cōram, *adv.*, face to face, openly

corium, -iī, *n.*, thick skin, hide

corolla, -ae, *f.*, small wreath of flowers, garland

corōna, -ae, *f.*, wreath of flowers

corpus, -oris, *n.*, body

cossim, *adv.*, squatting, crouching

costa, -ae, *f.*, rib

cōtīdiānus, -a, -um, *adj.*, daily, habitual

crassō (1), to thicken (hapax)

crassus, -a, -um, *adj.*, thick

crēber, -bra, -brum, *adj.*, frequent

crēbrescō, -ere, crēbruī, —, to become widespread, increase

crēdō, -ere, crēdidī, crēditum, to believe, consider

crescō, -ere, crēvī, crētum, to increase, grow

crīnis, -is, *m.*, a lock of hair

cruciābilis, -e, *adj.,*
excruciating, agonizing

cruciō (1), to torture, inflict
mental anguish

crūdēlitās, -ātis, *f.,* cruelty,
savagery

cruor, -ōris, *m.,* blood (from a
wound)

crūs, -ūris, *n.,* leg, shin

cubiculum, -ī, *n.,* a sleeping
apartment, bedroom

cubitum, -ī, *n.,* the elbow

cubō, -āre, -uī, -itum, to lie
down, sleep

culmen, -inis, *n.,* summit,
height, peak

cultus, -ūs, *m.,* veneration,
form of worship, observance

cum, *prep.* + *abl.,* with

cum, *conj.,* when, since,
although, after

cunctus, -a, -um, *adj.,* the
whole, all

Cupīdō, -inis, *m.,* Cupid, son of
Venus

cupīdo, -inis, *m.,* desire

cupidus, -a, -um, *adj.,* eager,
desirous, greedy

cupiō, -ere, -īvī *or* **-iī, -ītum,** to
desire, long for

cupītus, -a, -um, *adj.,* much
desired; *as substantive,* one's
desire

cūriōsē, *adv.,* carefully, curiously

cūriōsitās, -ātis, *f.,*
inquisitiveness, curiosity

cūriōsus, -a, -um, *adj.,* careful,
inquisitive, curious, nosey,
eager for knowledge

cutis, -is, *f.,* skin, hide

Cythēra, -ōrum, *n. pl.,*
Cythera, an island in the
Aegean sacred to Venus

dē, *prep.* + *abl.,* down from,
from, about

dea, -ae, *f.,* goddess

dēbeō, -ēre, -uī, -itum, to owe,
be under an obligation,
ought

dēbilis, -e, *adj.,* crippled,
weakened, feeble

dēcantō (1), to sing, bewitch

decenter, *adv.,* becomingly,
gracefully, decently

dēcernō, -ere, -crēvī, -crētum,
to resolve, decree

dēcipiō, -ere, -cēpī, -ceptum,
to deceive, disappoint,
cheat

decoriter, *adv.,* elegantly,
gracefully (first in Apuleius)

decuriō, -ōnis, *m.,* a member of
a governing committee of a
collegium

dēcurrō, -ere, -currī, -cursum,
to run down, hurry

dēdūcō, -ere, -duxī, -ductum,
to lead away, take along

dēficiō, -ere, -fēcī, -fectum, to
fail, lose strength; (pass. +
abl.) to be left without, lack

dēfīgō, -ere, -fixī, -fixum,
to fix, render incapable
of thought or movement,
dumbfound

dēfluō, -ere, -fluxī, -fluxum, to
flow away, fall to the ground

dēformis, -e, *adj.,* misshapen, ugly, disfigured

dēformō (1), to disfigure, transform

dēfricō (1), to rub

dehinc, *adv.,* after this, next

dēiciō, -ere, -iēcī, -iectum, to cast down

dein. *See* **deinde**

deinde, *adv.,* afterward, then, next

dēlābor, -ī, -lapsus sum, to fall, drop, slip

dēlectātiō, -onis, *f.,* delight, enjoyment

dēlēniō, -īre, -iī, -ītum, to soothe, mollify

dēlīberō (1), to consider carefully

dēlībō (1), to take, remove

dēlibūtus, -a, -um, *adj.,* smeared with, overflowing (+ abl.)

dēlicātus, -a, -um, *adj.,* dainty, pretty, elegant

dēlūbrum, -ī, *n.,* a temple, shrine

dēmergō, -ere, -mersī, -mersum, to submerge, plunge

dēmorsicō (1), to nibble (only in Apuleius)

dēmussō (1), to swallow in silence (first in Apuleius)

dēnique, *adv.,* finally, in short, and then, indeed

dens, -ntis, *m.,* tooth

densitās, -ātis, *f.,* thickness, density, abundance

deosculor, -ārī, -ātus sum, to kiss warmly

dēpellō, -ere, -pulī, -pulsum, to drive away, remove

dēpendulus, -a, -um, *adj.,* hanging down (only in Apuleius)

dēpingō, -ere, -pinxī, -pictum, to paint, color

dēplōrō (1), to lament, despair

dēprecor, -ārī, -ātus sum, to entreat, pray

dēprimō, -ere, -pressī, -pressum, to weigh down

dēprōmō, -ere, -prompsī, -promptum, to bring out

dēserviō, -īre, to devote oneself to, serve

dēsiderium, -iī, *n.,* a desire

dēsīdō, -ere, -sēdī, —, to sink, settle down

destinō (1), to determine, designate

destituō, -ere, -uī, -ūtum, to deprive of support, abandon

destringō, -ere, -strinxī, -strinctum, to draw (a weapon)

dēsultōrius, -a, -um, *adj.,* of a *desultor* (who jumps from one circus horse to another)

dētegō, -ere, -texī, -tectum, to uncover, reveal

dētergeō, -ēre, -tersī, -tersum, to wipe away

dēterior, -ius, *compar. adj.,* worse

dēterreō, -ēre, -uī, -itum, to deter, terrify

dētrīmentum, -ī, *n.,*
diminishment, loss, waning
(of moon)

dētrūdō, -ere, -trūsī, -trūsum,
to thrust off, push down,
reduce to

deus, -ī, *m.,* god

devestiō, -īre, + *abl.,* to
undress (only in Apuleius)

dēvolō (1), to fly away

dēvorō (1), to swallow, gulp
down

dexter, -era, -erum, *adj.,* on the
right, right

dextera, -ae, *f.,* the right hand

dicāculus, -a, -um, *adj.,*
talkative

dīcō, -ere, dīxī, dictum, to say,
speak, relate

dictō (1), to prescribe, dictate,
recommend

dictum, -ī, *n.,* what is said,
word

diēs, -ēī, *m./f.,* day

differō, -ferre, distulī,
dīlātum, to postpone,
defer

dīgerō, -ere, -gessī, -gestum, to
dissipate, dissolve

digitus, -ī, *m.,* finger, toe

dignitās, -ātis, *f.,* worthiness,
rank, status

dignor, -ārī, -ātus sum, to
consider worthy, deign,
think fit

dignus, -a, -um, *adj.,* worthy,
deserving

dīgredior, -ī, -gressus sum, to
go away, depart

dīligenter, *adv.,* carefully,
scrupulously

dīligentia, -ae, *f.,* carefulness,
attentiveness

dīlūculum, -ī, *n.,* dawn

dīmicō (1), to fight, contend

Diophanēs, -is, *m.,* Diophanes

dīrumpō, -ere, -rūpī, -ruptum,
to burst

dīrus, -a, -um, *adj.,* awful,
dreadful, frightful

discēdō, -ere, -cessī, -cessum,
to go off, go away

disciplīna, -ae, *f.,* instruction,
system, orderly conduct

discruciō (1), to torture, torment

discutiō, -ere, -cussī, -cussum,
to shake off

dispensō (1), to manage,
control, arrange

disputō (1), to argue, debate

dissēminātiō, -ōnis, *f.,* the
action of spreading abroad
(hapax)

disserō, -ere, -seruī, -sertum,
to say, discuss

distribuō, -ere, -tribuī,
-tribūtum, to divide up,
distribute

diū, *adv.,* for a long time

diūtinus, -a, -um, *adj.,* lasting
for a long time, long

dīversitās, -ātis, *f.,* difference,
diversity

dīversus, -a, -um, *adj.,* separate,
distant

dīvīnō (1), to interpret, guess,
know by intuition

dīvīnus, -a, -um, *adj.,* divine

dō, dare, dedī, datum, to give, grant, bestow

doctrīna, -ae, *f.*, teaching, learning

doleō, -ēre, -uī, -itum, to suffer, grieve

dolor, -ōris, *m.*, pain

dolus, -ī, *m.*, deception, trickery

domina, -ae, *f.*, mistress (of female heads of household or as goddess)

dominus, -ī, *m.*, master, lord; (as title) sir

domus, -ūs, *f.*, house; **domī,** at home; **domum,** (to) home

dormiō, -īre, -īvī or **-iī, -ītum,** to sleep

dorsum, -ī, *n.*, the back

dulcis, -e, *adj.*, sweet, dear, charming

dum, *conj.*, while, provided that, as long as

duo, -ae, -o, *adj.*, two

dūrō (1), to harden

dūrus, -a, -um, *adj.*, hard, harsh

ecce, *interj.*, behold!, look!, mark this!

ēdō, -ere, edidī, editum, to emit, bring forth, carry out, perform (actions)

edō, esse, ēdī, ēsum or **essum,** to eat

ēducō (1), to nurture, bring forth

efficio, -ere, -fēci, -factum, to make

effigiēs, -ēī, *f.*, a representation, image, shape

efflictim, *adv.*, passionately

effundō, -ere, -fūdī, -fūsum, to pour out, stream forth

ēgerō, -ere, egessī, egestum, to carry out, remove

ego, *pron.*, I

egomet, *pron.*, (intensive of **ego**; acc. *memet*)

ēgregius, -ia, -ium, *adj.*, outstanding, extraordinary

ēiulō, -āre, —, —, to shriek, wail

ēlābor, -ī, elapsus sum, to slip, slide, steal away

elementum, -ī, *n.*, one of the four substances from which all matter was said to be made, an element

Eleusīnius, -a, -um, *adj.*, Eleusinian, from Eleusis (where the mysteries of Demeter are celebrated)

ēlevō (1), to lift, raise

ēmergō, -ere, ēmersī, ēmersum, to come up out of the water, emerge, get up

ēminus, *adv.*, at long range

emptor, -ōris, *m.*, a buyer

ēn, *interj.*, look!, observe! (often ironical)

enim, *confirming and emphatic particle,* indeed, of course, truly

enimvērō, *particle,* truly!, certainly

ēnixē, *adv.*, strenuously, assidously

ēnormis, -e, *adj.*, abnormally large, enormous

eō, īre, īvī *or* **iī, itum,** to go, proceed, come

Ephesus, -ī, *m.*, Ephesus, a city in Asia Minor famous for its worship of Diana

Ephyrēus, -a, -um, *adj.*, Corinthian

epulō, -ōnis, *m.*, a banqueter, diner

epulum, -ī, *n.* feast

equidem, *particle*, for my part, in truth

equus, -ī, *m.*, horse

ērigō, -ere, ērexī, ērectum, to raise up, lift

et, *conj.*, and, as well

etiam, *particle*, still, even, also

etsī, *conj.*, even if, although

ēvidens, *gen.* **-ntis,** *adj.*, clear, obvious

ēvigilō (1), to wake up

ēvincō, -ere, ēvīcī, ēvictum, to defeat utterly

ēvolō (1), to fly away, rush out

ēvomō, -ere, -uī, -itum, to spew out

ex, *prep.* + *abl.*, from, out of

exanclō (1), to endure

exanimō (1), to destroy, exhaust

exaptō (1), to place on (hapax)

exardescō, -ere, -arsī, -arsum, to catch fire, to blaze with passion

exasperō (1), to make sore, irritate

exciō, -īre, -īvī, -ītum, to summon, give rise to

excolō, -ere, -coluī, -cultum, to cultivate, develop

exemplum, -ī, *n.*, example, case, precedent

exeō, - īre, -īvī, -itum, to come or go out

exercitātus, -a, -um, *adj.*, practiced, versed

exhibeō, -ēre, -uī, -itum, to produce, show, present, provide

exiguus, -a, -um, *adj.*, small, short

exiliō, -īre, -uī, —, to leap up

eximiē, *adv.*, especially, exceptionally

eximius, -a, -um, *adj.*, exceptional

exin, *adv.*, thereafter, next

exitium, -ī, *n.*, destruction, ruin

exoptō (1), to long for

exordior, -īrī, -orsus sum, to begin (in weaving, to lay the warp)

exordium, -iī, *n.*, beginning

exorior, -īrī, -ortus sum, to arise, come into existence

exōticus, -a, -um, *adj.*, coming from overseas, foreign

expediō, -īre, -īvī *or* **-iī, -ītum,** to extricate, explain, narrate

expergiscor, -ī, experrectus sum, to wake up

expleō, -ēre, -plēvī, -plētum, to fill up

explicō, -āre, -uī, -ātum *or* **-itum,** to give an account, carry out explōrō (1), to inspect

expostulō (1), to complain, remonstrate

exprimō, -ere, -pressī, -pressum, to express

exsequor, -ī, -secūtus sum, to pursue, execute (a duty)

exsolvō, -ere, -soluī, -solūtum, to unfasten, unload

exspectātiō, -ōnis, f., suspense, waiting

exsurgō, -ere, -surrexī, —, to rise

exterminō (1), to send beyond a boundary, expel

exterō, -ere, -terīvī, -terītum, to wear down, rub away

extimescō, -ere, -timuī, to be afraid, be alarmed

extimus, -a, -um, adj., outermost, furthest

extinguō, -ere, -tinxī, -tinctum, to exstinguish, annihilate

extrēmus, -a, -um, adj., outermost, extreme, distressing

exulcerō (1), to make sore, inflame

exurgō, See exsurgō

fābula, -ae, f., talk, conversation, tale, story

facessō, -ere, -īvī or -iī, -ītum, go away, depart

faciēs, -iēī, f., appearance, look, face

facilis, -e, adj., easy

facilitās, -ātis, f., ease

facinerōsus, -a, -um, adj., criminal, wicked

facinus, -oris, n., deed, crime

faciō, -ere, fēcī, factum, to make, do

factum, -ī, n., deed, action

fallō, -ere, fefellī, falsum, to deceive

fāma, -ae, f., news, report, rumor

famēs, -is, f., hunger

fāmigerābilis, -e, adj., famous (only here and in Varro)

familia, -ae, f., household, family, slaves of a household

familiāris, -e, adj., familiar, habitual

famula, -ae, f., serving-woman

famulus, -ī, m., servant, slave

farīnulentus, -a, -um, adj., floury (hapax)

fartim, adv., densely

fās, indecl., n., what is morally right, fitting or proper

fasceola, -ae, f., band, ribbon, breast band

fatīgō (1), to tire out, exhaust

fātum, -ī, m., fate, Fate (personified), destiny

faustus, -a, -um, adj., fortunate, favorable

faveō, -ēre, fāvī, fautum, to favor, be propitious (+ dat.)

fēlīciter, adv., fortunately

fēlix, gen. -icis, adj., blessed, fertile, lucky

fēmina, -ae, f., woman

fēmineus, -a, -um, adj., feminine

fenestra, -ae, *f.,* window

fera, -ae, *f.,* a wild animal

fērālis, -e, *adj.,* funereal, death-bringing

ferīnus, -a, -um, *adj.,* of wild beasts, bestial

feriō, -īre, —, —, to strike, knock

fermē, *adv.,* approximately, about

ferrum, -ī, *n.,* sword

fervens, *gen.* **-ntis,** *adj.,* intensely hot

festīnanter, *adv.,* quickly

festīnātiō, -ōnis, *f.,* speed, haste

festīnō (1), to hurry

festīnus, -a, -um, *adj.,* quick, impatient

festīvē, *adv.,* delightfully, prettily

fētus, -a, -um, *adj.,* having recently given birth

fidēs, -ēī, *f.,* trust, good faith, honesty

Fidēs, -ēī, *f.,* the deity Fides

fīgō, -ere, fixī, fixum, to fix in position, make motionless or rigid, fix

figura, -ae, *f.,* form, shape, figure

fīlia, -ae, *f.,* daughter

fīnis, -is, *m./f.,* end, limit, boundary

fīō, fīērī, factus sum, to be made, become

firmiter, *adv.,* resolutely

fistula, -ae, *f.,* pan-pipe

flāgitium, -iī, disgrace, shameful deed

flāgitō (1), to ask, demand

flāmen, -inis, *n.,* wind, breeze

flēbilis, -e, *adj.,* worthy of tears, causing tears, tearful

flectō, -ere, flexī, flexum, to bend

fleō, -ēre, flēvī, flētum, to weep, lament

flētus, -ūs, *m.,* weeping, lamentation

flexus, -ūs, *m.,* the act of bending, curving, turning

flōreō, -ēre, -uī, to blossom, flourish, excel

flōrescō, -ere, to blossom, increase in renown

flōridus, -a, -um, *adj.,* flowery, pretty

flōs, -ōris, *m.,* flower, bloom, luster

fluctuō (1), to undulate, hesitate

fluctus, -ūs, *m.,* wave

fluō, -ere, fluxī, fluxum, to flow, originate

foculus, -ī, *m.,* stove, brazier

foedō (1), to make filthy, stain

foliātus, -a, -um, *adj.,* endowed with leaves

follicō, -āre, —, —, to hang loosely, sag (hapax)

fontānus, -a, -um, *adj.,* of a fountain or spring

forāmen, -inis, *n.,* hole

forensis, -e, *adj.,* of the Forum, connected to the law courts, (*possibly*) foreign

forinsecus, *adv.,* out, away

foris, -is, *f.,* door

forma, -ae, *f.*, appearance, beauty

formīdō, -inis, *f.*, fear

formonsē, *adv.*, beautifully

formonsitās, -ātis, *f.*, beauty

formonsus, -a, -um, *adj.*, beautiful, handsome

forte, *adv.*, by chance

fortis, -e, *adj.*, strong, powerful

fortūna, -ae, *f.*, fortune, chance, misfortune, circumstance

Fortūna, -ae, *f.*, the goddess, Fortune

forum, -ī, *n.*, public square, the Roman Forum

Fōtis, -idis, *f.*, Fotis, slave of Milo (also **Photis**)

fraglō (1), to burn, burn with passion

fraus, -dis, *f.*, deceit, deception

fremō, -ere, -uī, -itum, to grumble, mutter, growl

frequens, *gen.* -ntis, *adj.*, crowded, multitudinous, repeated

frīgidus, -a, -um, *adj.*, cold

frons, -ntis, *f.*, the forehead, brow

fructus, -ūs, *m.*, fruit, profit, reward

frustātim, *adv.*, in little pieces

frustrā, *adv.*, in vain

frux, -ūgis, *f.*, fruit; **bonae frugi esse,** to be good, do the right thing

fuga, -ae, *f.*, flight

fulgurō (1), to glitter, gleam

fūmōsus, -a, -um, *adj.*, smoky

fundāmentum, -ī, *n.*, foundation

fūnestus, -a, -um, *adj.*, deathly, grievous

furcifer, -erī, *m.*, scoundrel, villain

furens, *gen.* -ntis, *adj.*, frenzied

furor, -ōris, *m.*, fury, rage

fustis, -is, *m.*, stick, rod

gaudeō, -ēre, gāvīsus sum, to be glad, rejoice

gaudium, -iī, *n.*, joy

gelidus, -a, -um, *adj.*, cold, icy

gena, -ae, *f.*, cheek

generō (1), to beget, create

geniālis, -e, *adj.*, nuptial, festive, delightful, joyous

geniāliter, *adv.*, with good cheer, in a convivial manner

genu, -ūs, *n.*, knee

genus, -eris, *n.*, descent, offspring, race, kind

germen, -inis, *n.*, a shoot, sprout

gerō, -ere, gessī, gestum, bear, perform

gerula, -ae, *f.*, a carrier, porter

gestiō, -īre, -īvī *or* -iī, to be eager, desire eagerly, make a gesture

gestus, -ūs, *m.*, movement, gesture

glabellus, -a, -um, *adj.*, hairless, smooth (only in Apuleius)

gladius, -iī, *m.*, a sword

glans, -ndis, *f.*, acorn

glēba, -ae, *f.*, clod of earth, land

globus, -ī, *m.,* dense mass

glōria, -ae, *f.,* praise, honor, glory

glōriōsus, -a, -um, *adj.,* illustrious

grabattus, -ī, *m.,* bed, couch

Graecānicus, -a, -um, *adj.,* Greekish, Greek in origin but adapted for Latin use

Grāius, -a, -um, *adj.,* Greek, a Greek

grandis, -e, *adj.,* large

grātia, -iae, *f.,* favor, thanks

Grātiae, -ārum, *f. pl.,* the three Graces, goddesses embodying charm

grātulor, -ārī, -ātus sum, to give thanks, congratulate, be glad

grātus, -a, -um, *adj.,* grateful, attractive, pleasing

gravis, -e, *adj.,* heavy

gremium, -iī, *n.,* lap, bosom

grex, -egis, *m.* an assembly, crowd

gutta, -ae, *f.,* a drop

habeō, -ēre, -uī, -itum, to have, possess

habitātiō, -ōnis, *f.,* lodging

haereō, -ēre, haesī, haesum, to be unable to move, to stick to a spot

hauriō, -īre, hausī, hauritum, to scoop up

haustus, -ūs, *m.,* a drink, gulp

hēiulō, -āre, —, —, to shriek, wail

hem, *interj.,* what's that?, ah!

heus, *interj.,* hey!

hic, haec, hoc, *pron., adj.,* this, he, she, it

hilarō (1), to cheer, gladden

hiō, -āre, -āvī, —, to gape, be wide open

hiulcus, -a, -um, *adj.,* gaping, distended

homō, -inis, *m.,* a human being, person

homunculus, -ī, *m.,* a worthless person

honor, -ōris, *m.,* mark of esteem, honor

Hōrae, -ārum, *f. pl.,* goddesses of the seasons

horrendus, -a, -um, *adj.,* terrible, fearful

horridus, -a, -um, *adj.,* rough, dishevelled

horripilō, -āre, —, —, to become bristly

hospes, -itis, *m.,f.,* host

hospita, -ae, *f.,* female host

hospitālis, -e, *adj.,* of or belonging to hospitality

hospitium, -iī, *n.,* house, home

hūmānē, *adv.,* befitting a human, in a friendly manner

hūmānitās, -ātis, *f.,* human nature, human feeling

hūmānus, -a, -um, *adj.,* human

humilis, -e, *adj.,* humble, low, low down

Hymettos, -ī (Greek forms), *f.,* Hymettus, a mountain in Attica

iaceō, -ēre, -uī, -itum, to lie down, lie
iam, *adv.,* now, already, soon
iānua, -ae, *f.,* door
ibī, *adv.,* there
ibīdem, *adv.,* in that same place
ictus, -ūs, *m.,* a blow
identidem, *adv.,* repeatedly
idōneē, *adv.,* adequately
idōneus, -a, -um, *adj.,* adequate, appropriate
ignārus, -a, -um, *adj.,* unaware, ignorant
igniculus, -ī, *m.,* a small fire
ignis, -is, *m.,* fire, light
īlicō, *adv.,* on the spot, then and there
ille, -a, -ud, *pron., adj.,* that, he, she, it, the
illīc, *adv.,* there
illūc, *adv.,* to that place
illūminō (1), to illuminate, throw light on
imāginābundus, -a, -um, *adj.,* picturing to oneself (hapax)
imāgō, -inis, *f.,* likeness, representation, picture, image, shape, appearance
immensus, -a, -um, *adj.,* huge, immeasurable, immense
immergō, -ere, -mersī, -mersum, to dip, plunge
imminuō, -ere, -minuī, -minūtum, to reduce in size, diminish
immittō, -ere, -mīsī, -missum, to insert, lay on

immō, *particle,* (correcting a previous statement) rather
immōbilis, -e, *adj.,* motionless
immortālis, -e, *adj,* immortal, deathless
immūtātiō, -ōnis, *f.,* alteration, change
impediō, -īre, -īvī, -ītum, to restrict, bind, clasp
impertior, -īrī, —, —, to give, bestow
impetus, -ūs, *m.,* attack
implectō, -ere, -plexī, -plexum, to intertwine
impos, *gen.* **-otis,** *adj.,* not having control; **impos animī,** out of one's mind
īmus, -a, -um, *adj.,* lowest
in, *prep.,* (+ abl.) in, on, at; (+ acc.) into, onto
inaccessus, -a, -um, *adj.,* unapproachable, unequaled
inanimus, -a, -um, *adj.,* inanimate
incēdō, -ere, -cessī, —, to walk
incendō, -ere, -cendī, -censum, to inflame, provoke
inceptum, -ī, *n.,* an undertaking, start
incertus, -a, -um, *adj.,* uncertain, variable, fluctuating
incidō, -ere, -cidī, -casum, to fall
incipiō, -ere, -cēpī, -ceptum, to begin
inclitus, -a, -um, *adj.,* famous, celebrated

incorōnātus, -a, -um, *adj.*, not crowned with garlands

incrēbrescō, -ere, -crebruī, —, to increase, become stronger

incrēmentum, -ī, *n.*, increase, waxing (of moon)

incunctanter, *adv.*, unhesitatingly

incurvus, -a, -um, *adj.*, curved, bent

inde, *adv.*, from that place

indicō (1), to reveal, declare

indidem, *adv.*, from that same place or source

indigena, -ae, *m.*, one born in a place, a native; *attrib.*: native

indignātiō, -ōnis, *f.*, anger, indignation

indignē, *adv.*, undeservedly

indiguus, -a, -um, *adj.*, having need of

indūcō, -ere, -duxī, -ductum, to lead

ineptus, -a, -um, *adj.*, foolish

inequitō, -āre, —, —, to ride into

inerrō (1), to wander or roam in

inexōrābilis, -e, *adj.*, inexorable, relentless

infēlix, *gen.* **-īcis,** *adj.*, unlucky, unhappy

inferī, -ōrum, *m. pl.*, the inhabitants of the underworld, the dead

infernus, -a, -um, *adj.*, of the underworld, infernal

infestus, -a, -um, *adj.*, hostile

infirmus, -a, -um, *adj.*, weak

inflō (1), to blow into (an instrument), to inflate

ingemescō, -ere, -gemuī, —, to groan, groan about

ingens, *gen.* **-ntis,** *adj.*, huge, very great

ingerō, -ere, -gessī, -gestum, to heap on

ingignō, -ere, -genuī, -genitum, to grow in, be inborn

ingrātīs, *f. abl. pl. of* **ingratia** *used adverbially,* against one's wishes

ingredior, -ī, -gressus sum, to enter, go forward

inhaereō, -ēre, -haesī, -haesum, to remain fixed

inhiō (1), to gaze at eagerly, to gaze with longing

iniciō, -ere, -iēcī, -iectum, to lay on, (pf. pple. + abl.) clothed in, covered with

initiālis, -e, *adj.*, original, primary

initium, -iī, *n.*, start, beginning

iniūria, -ae, *f.*, a wrong, injustice

inlicitus, -a, -um, *adj.*, forbidden

inlubricans, *gen.* **-antis,** *adj.*, sinuously moving (hapax)

inlūcescō, -ere, —, —, to shine on, to grow light

inlustris, -e, *adj.*, bright, illustrious

inmeritō, *adv.*, unjustly

inmodicus, -a, -um, *adj.*,
excessive, extravagant

innocens, *gen.* -ntis, *adj.*,
innocent

innoxius, -a, -um, *adj.*,
harmless

inopia, -ae, *f.*, lack of means,
dearth, helplessness

inoptābilis, -e, *adj.*,
undesirable, unpleasant

inpatiens, *gen.* -ntis, *adj.* + *gen.*,
not tolerating

inpatientia, -ae, *f.*,
unwillingness to endure (a
situation)

inprosperus, -a, -um, *adj.*, ill-
starred, unfortunate

inprōvidus, -a, -um, *adj.*,
thoughtless, unforeseeing

inquam, —, —, —, to say

inquiētus, -a, -um, *adj.*,
restless, ceaseless

inremūnerābilis, -e, *adj.*, that
cannot be repaid (hapax)

inrēpō, -ere, -repsī, —, to creep
in

inruptiō, -ōnis, *f.*, forcible
entry, incursion

insatiābilis, -e, *adj.*, insatiable

inscrībō, -ere, -scripsī,
-scriptum, to write, inscribe

insequor (insecor), -ī, -secūtus
sum, to follow, chase, attack

insideō, -ēre, -sēdī, -sessum, to
sit, be seated

insidiae, -ārum, *f. pl.*, trap, snare

insigne, -is, *n.*, an outward
signal or token of rank,
decoration

insistō, -ere, institī, —, to halt,
come to a standstill

insonus, -a, -um, *adj.*, silent

inspiciō, -ere, -spexī, -spectum,
to examine, look at

instans, *gen.* -ntis, *adj.*, urgent

instaurō (1), to repeat, start
anew

instruō, -ere, -strūxī,
-structum, to furnish,
provide

insula, -ae, *f.*, island

insum, inesse, infuī, —, to be
present in

intellegō, -ere, -lēxī, -lectum,
to understand

intendō, -ere, -tendī, -tentum,
to direct one's attention

inter, *prep.* + *acc.*, between,
among, during

interdum, *adv.*, meanwhile

intereā, *adv.*, meanwhile

interim, *adv.*, for the time

intexō, -ere, -texuī, -textum, to
weave into, weave together

intimus, -a, -um, *adj.*, inmost,
deepest

intingō, -ere, -tinxī, -tinctum,
to dip in

intorqueō, -ēre, -torsī,
-tortum, to twist, turn,
spin

intueor, -ērī, -tuitus sum, to
gaze at, watch

intus, *adv.*, inside

inumbrō (1), to cast a shadow,
shade

inūrō, -ere, -ussī, -ustum,
burn, scorch

invādō, -ere, -vāsī, -vāsum, to enter, seize

inveniō, -īre, -vēnī, -ventum, to discover, encounter

invidia, -ae, *f.,* jealousy, ill-will

invītus, -a, -um, *adj.,* unwilling

invocō (1), to address

iocor, -ārī, -ātus sum, to jest, joke

ipse, ipsa, ipsum, *pron., adj.,* himself, herself, itself

is, ea, id, *pron., adj.,* he, she, it, this, that

Īsis, -idis, *f.,* Isis

iste, ista, istud, *pron., adj.,* that, he, she, it

Isthmos, -ī (Greek forms), *f.,* the isthmus of Corinth

itaque, *adv.,* consequently, and so

iter, -ineris, *n.,* journey

iubar, -aris, *n.,* radiance, sunlight

iubeō, -ēre, iussī, iussum, to order

iūdex, -icis, *m./f.,* judge, juror

iūdicium, -iī, *n.,* trial, judgment

iugulō (1), to kill, slaughter

iūmentārius, -a, -um, *adj.,* related to beasts of burden, beastly

iūmentum, -ī, *n.,* beast of burden

iūnior, -oris, *compar. adj.,* younger

Iūnō, -ōnis, *f.,* Juno, wife and sister of Juppiter

Iuppiter, Iovis, *m.,* Jupiter, king of the gods

iūrulentus, -a, -um, *adj.,* juicy, stewed

iūs, iūris, *n.,* law, bonds (arising out of a given social relationship)

iussus, -ūs, *m.,* command

iustitia, -ae, *f.,* justice

iuvenis, -is, *m.,* a young man, young person

labia, -ae, *n.,* lip

labor, -ōris, *m.,* work, toil, hardship

labōriōsus, -a, -um, *adj.,* involving much labor, painful

lacertus, -ī, *m.,* the upper arm

lacinia, -ae, *f.,* a garment, strip of cloth

lacrima, -ae, *f.,* a tear, weeping

lacrimōsus, -a, -um, *adj.,* tearful

lacteus, -a, -um, *adj.,* milky, milky white

lacūnar, -āris, *n.,* panelled ceiling, one of the panels of a ceiling

laetitia, -ae, *f.,* joy, happiness, pleasure

laetō (1), to gladden, cheer

laetor, -ārī, -ātus sum, to rejoice, be glad, be delighted

laetus, -a, -um, *adj.,* happy, joyous, fertile

lāmentātiō, -ōnis, *f.,* wailing, lamentation

languidus, -a, -um, *adj.*, weary, drooping

lapideus, -a, -um, *adj.*, made of stone

lapis, -idis, *m.*, stone

larvālis, -e, *adj.*, ghostlike, deathly

lascīviō, -īre, -iī, -ītum, to frolic, behave lasciviously

lassitūdō, -inis, *f.*, tiredness

lassus, -a, -um, *adj.*, weary

latex, -icis, *m.*, water, liquid

Latius, -a, -um, *adj.*, of Latium, Roman

lātrātus, -ūs, *m.*, barking

latrō, -ōnis, *m.*, robber, brigand

lātus, -eris, *n.*, the side

laudō (1), to praise

laus, -dis, *f.*, praise, commendation

lautia, -ōrum, *n. pl.*, entertainment provided for foreign guests at Rome

lavācrum, -ī, *n.*, bath

lavō, -āre *or* -ere, lāvī, lavātum *or* lautum, to wash

lector, -ōris, *m.*, reader

lectulus, -ī, *m.*, couch

lēgātiō, -ōnis, *f.*, embassy

lēniō, -īre, -īvī, -ītum, to soothe, comfort, soften

lēniter, *adv.*, gently

lepidus, -a, -um, *adj.*, charming, witty, amusing

levis, -e, *adj.*, light, fickle

lex, lēgis, *f.*, law

libenter, *adv.*, gladly

Līber, -erī, *m.*, Bacchus

liber, -brī, *m.*, book

līberē, *adv.*, freely

līberō (1), to set free, release, deliver

lībertus, -ī, *m.*, freedman

lībrō (1), to make horizontal, poise, balance (of aerial flight)

licet, -ēre, licuit *or* licitum est, it is permitted; although

lictor, -ōris, *m.*, lictor, attendant to a Roman magistrate

līneus, -a, -um, *adj.*, made of linen or flax

lingua, -ae, *f.*, tongue, language

litō (1), to make a sacrifice or offering, propitiate (+ dat.)

litterātus, -a, -um, *adj.*, inscribed with letters, tattooed

līvidus, -a, -um, *adj.*, livid, black and blue

locus, -ī, *m.*, *or* locum, -ī, *n.*, place

locūtor, -ōris, *m.*, a speaker, talker

longē, *adv.*, very, very much

longus, -a, -um, *adj.*, long

loquor, -ī, locūtus sum, to talk, speak

lūbricus, -a, -um, *adj.*, slippery, loose, hazardous

lucerna, -ae, *f.*, lamp

Lūcius, -ī, *m.*, Lucius

luctor, -ārī, -ātus sum, to wrestle

lūculentus, -a, -um, *adj.*, splendid, beautiful

lūcus, -ī, *m.*, grove, wood
lūdicer, -cra, -crum, *adj.*,
    playful
lūgubriter, *adv.*, mournfully
    (hapax)
lumbus, -ī, *m.*, lower body,
    loins
lūmen, -inis, *n.*, light, eye,
    spout
lūminātus, -a, -um, *adj.*,
    having sight
lūminōsus, -a, -um, *adj.*,
    gleaming
lūna, -ae, *f.*, moon
lupula, -ae, *f.*, she-wolf
lupus, -ī, *m.*, wolf
lūror, -ōris, *m.*, pallor
lūsus, -ūs, *m.*, game, joke,
    public festival
lux, lūcis, *f.*, light

machaera, -ae, *f.*, sword
maciēs, -ēī, *f.*, thinness,
    wasting
Madaurensis, -is, *adj.*, from
    Madauros in North Africa
maereō, -ēre, to mourn
maeror, -ōris, *m.*, grief, sorrow
maestus, -a, -um, *adj.*, sad,
    mournful
magicus, -a, -um, *adj.*,
    concerned with magic,
    magic
magis, *adv.*, more
magister, -trī, *m.*, teacher
magisterium, -iī, *n.*,
    instruction
magistrātus, -ūs, *m.*,
    magistrate

magnificentia, -ae, *f.*,
    greatness, splendor
magnus, -a, -um, *adj.*, great
māiestās, -ātis, *f.*, greatness,
    majesty
maior, -or, -us, *compar. adj.*
    of magnus, greater; (as
    substantive) ancestors
male, *adv.*, badly
malevolus, -a, -um, *adj.*,
    spiteful, malevolent
malitia, -ae, *f.*, wicked
    character, wickedness
mancipium, -iī, *n.*, the legal
    claiming of property, slave
mandō (1), to commit,
    command, assign
mānēs, -ium, *m. pl.*, shades of
    the dead
manifestus, -a, -um, *adj.*,
    visible
mansiō, -ōnis, *f.*, dwelling
manus, -ūs, *f.*, hand
marcidus, -a, -um, *adj.*,
    exhausted, weak
mare, -is, *n.*, the sea
marīnus, -a, -um, *adj.*, of the
    sea, marine
marītus, -ī, *m.*, husband
māter, -tris, *f.*, mother
materiēs, -ēī, *f.*, substance,
    object
māternus, -a, -um, *adj.*,
    maternal, motherly
mātūrus, -a, -um, *adj.*, ripe,
    ripe for delivery
mātūtīnus, -a, -um, *adj.*,
    belonging to the morning,
    morning

maximus, -a, -um, *adj.*, greatest
meātus, -ūs, *m.*, movement, path
medēla, -ae, *f.*, treatment, cure
medius, -a, -um, *adj.*, middle
melior, *gen.* **-oris,** *compar. adj. of* **bonus,** better
mellītula, -ae, *f.*, sweetheart, honey (hapax)
mellītus, -a, -um, *adj.*, honey-sweet
membrum, -ī, *n.*, part of the body, limb
memet. *See* **egomet**
meminī, -inisse, to remember
memorō (1), to speak, narrate
mens, -tis, *f.*, the mind
mensa, -ae, *f.*, table
mensūra, -ae, *f.*, measure, extent
mentior, -īrī, -ītus sum, to lie, fabricate
mercēs, -ēdis, *f.*, payment
Mercurius, -ī, *m.*, Mercury
mereō, -ēre, -uī, -itum, earn, acquire
mereor, -ērī, -itum. *See* **mereō**
merīdiēs, -ēī, *m./f.*, noon, afternoon
mēta, -ae, *f.*, limit, end, turning-point
metuō, -ere, metuī, metūtum, to fear
metus, -ūs, *m./f.*, fear
meus, -a, -um, *adj.*, my, mine
micō, -āre, -uī, —, to throb, palpitate
Mīlēsius, -a, -um, *adj.*, Milesian, from Miletus in Asia Minor

mille, *indecl. pl.*, **milia,** *adj.*, thousand
Milō, -ōnis, *m.*, Milo, Lucius' host
minister, -trī, *m.*, servant, assistant
ministerium, -iī, *n.*, servant, attendant, instrument, tool
ministrō (1), to serve, provide, administer
minus, *compar. adv.*, less, not so
minūtiēs, -ēī, *f.*, smallness
mīrābilis, -e, *adj.*, marvelous, wondrous
mīrābundus, -a, -um, *adj.*, astonished at
mīror, -ārī, -ātus sum, to be amazed, wonder at
mīrus, -a, -um, *adj.*, extraordinary
miscellāneus, -a, -um, *adj.*, mixed
misellus, -a, -um, *adj.*, poor, wretched, pitiable
miser, -era, -erum, *adj.*, poor, wretched, unfortunate
miserātiō, -ōnis, *f.*, compassion, pity
misericordia, -ae, *f.*, compassion
Misericordia, -ae, *f.*, Compassion (personified)
miseror, -ārī, -ātus, to feel pity or compassion
missiō, -ōnis, *f.*, release
mītis, -e, *adj.*, gentle, mild, cultivated
mittō, -ere, mīsī, missum, to send, let go, stop

mōbilis, -e, *adj.,* quick, nimble
modicē, *adv.,* moderately
modo, *adv.,* only; **modo si,**
    provided that
modus, -ī, *m.,* manner
moenia, -ium, *n. pl.,* walls
mōlēs, -is, *f.,* a mass, vast
    amount of
mollis, -e, *adj.,* soft
moneō, -ēre, -uī, -itum, to
    warn
monitus, -ūs, *m.,* warning,
    advice, counsel
monstrō (1), to show, designate
monstrum, -ī, *n.,* a portent,
    prodigy
mora, -ae, *f.,* delay
mordicus, *adv.,* with the teeth,
    by biting
morior, -ī, mortuus sum, to
    die
moror, -ārī, -ātus sum, to delay
mors, -tis, *f.,* death
mortālis, -e, *adj.,* mortal
mortuus, -a, -um, *adj.,* dead
mōs, mōris, *m.,* custom, habit,
    style
mox, *adv.,* soon, next
mulier, -eris, *f.,* woman
mulsum, -ī, *n.,* wine mixed
    with honey, mead
multiformis, -e, *adj.,* many-
    shaped, multiform
multiiugus, -a, -um, *adj.,* yoked
    many together, having many
    parts, many and varied
multiscius, -a, -um, *adj.,*
    having much knowledge
    (only in Apuleius)

multivius, -a, -um, *adj.,* making
    many rounds (hapax)
multō (1), to punish
multus, -a, -um, *adj.,* much,
    many
mūlus, -ī, *m.,* mule
mundulē, *adv.,* elegantly (only
    in Accius and Apuleius)
mūnia, -ōrum, *n. pl.,* official
    duties, functions
mūnus, -eris, *n.,* task, duty, gift
murmur, -uris, *n.,* a hum,
    murmur, whisper
Mūsa, -ae, *f.,* a muse, goddess of
    the arts
mūsica, -ae, *f.,* music
mūtātiō, -ōnis, *f.,* change,
    transformation
mūtō (1), to change
mūtus, -a, -um, *adj.,* mute,
    unspeaking
mūtuus, -a, -um, *adj.,*
    reciprocal, mutual

nam, *conj.,* for
namque, *conj.,* for
nanciscor, -ī, nactus *or* **nanctus
    sum,** to find, arrive at, meet
    with
nāris, -is, *f.,* the nose, *pl.* nostrils
nascor, -ī, nātus sum, to be
    born
nāsus, -ī, *m.,* the nose
nātālis, -is, *m.,* birth, origin
nates, -ium, *f. pl.,* the buttocks
nātīvus, -a, -um, *adj.,* native,
    local
nātūra, -ae, *f.,* nature, private
    parts

nātūrālis, -e, *adj.,* natural
nāvigō (1), to sail, go by ship
nāvita, -ae, *m.,* sailor
nāviter, *adv.,* diligently
nē, *adv. and conj.,* so that not, lest, (with understood *quidem*) not even
nebula, -ae, *f.,* cloud
nec, *conj.,* nor, and not; **nec . . . nec,** neither . . . nor
necessitās, -ātis, *f.,* necessity, constraint
neclegō, -ere, -lexī, -lectum, to neglect, disregard
necō (1), to kill
nectar, -aris, *n.,* the drink of the gods
nefārius, -a, -um, *adj.,* wicked
neglegō. *See* **neclegō**
negōtium, -iī, *n.,* business
nēmō, -inis, *m./f.,* nobody
nepōs, -ōtis, *m.,* nephew, descendant
nēquam, *indecl.,* bad; **nequissimus,** *superl.,* worthless
neque. *See* **nec**
nequeō, -īre, -īvī *or* **-iī, —,** to be unable
nesciō, -īre, -īvī *or* **-iī, -ītum,** to not know
nexus, -ūs, *m.,* bond, embrace, intertwining
nihil, *indecl.,* nothing
Nīlōticus, -a, -um, *adj.,* Nilotic (of the Nile)
nimietās, -ātis, *f.,* excess
nimiō, *adv.,* too much, excessively

nīmīrum, *particle,* evidently (ironic)
nimis, *adv.,* too, too much, very
nimius, -a, -um, *adj.,* excessive, extraordinary
nisi, *conj.,* unless, if . . . not
nīsus, -ūs, *m.,* a pressing upon, pressure
nōbilitās, -ātis, *f.,* renown, distinction
nocturnus, -a, -um, *adj.,* nocturnal, belonging to the night
nōlō, nolle, noluī, —, to refuse, not want
nōmen, -inis, *n.,* name
nōminō (1), to name
nōn, *adv.,* not
nōnnullus, -a, -um, *adj.,* some
nōs, *pron.,* we, I
nōscō, -ere, nōvī, nōtum, to know how
noster, -tra, -trum, *adj.,* our
novācula, -ae, *f.,* a sharp knife, razor
novitās, -ātis, *f.,* novelty
novus, -a, -um, *adj.,* new
nox, -ctis, *f.,* night
noxius, -a, -um, *adj.,* harmful
nullus, -a, -um, *adj.,* no, none
nūmen, -inis, *n.,* divine power, deity
numerō (1), to count, reckon
numerus, -ī, *m.,* number
nunc, *adv.,* now
nuptiae, -ārum, *f. pl.,* marriage
nuptiālis, -e, *adj.,* nuptial

nusquam, *adv.*, nowhere
nūtriō, -īre, -īvī *or* **-iī, -ītum,** to feed, nourish
nūtus, -ūs, *m.*, nod, gesture of the head

ō, *interj.*, oh
ob, *prep.* + *acc.*, on account of, toward
obeō, -īre, -īvī *or* **-iī, -itum,** to perform, go or come, visit, meet, die
obēsus, -a, -um, *adj.*, fat
obitus, -ūs, *m.*, an encounter, visit
oblātiō, -ōnis, *f.*, an offering, presentation
oblīcus, -a, -um, *adj.*, at an angle
oblīquō (1), to cast sideways (of the eyes)
oboediō, -īre, -īvī *or* **-iī, -ītum,** to obey, act in accordance with the demands of a situation
oborior, -īrī, obortus sum, to spring up, be produced
obsequenter, *adv.*, obediently
obsequium, -iī, *n.*, service, servility
obserō (1), to bar off, obstruct
observō (1), to watch for
obsitus, -a, -um, *adj.*, covered with
obstinātus, -a, -um, *adj.*, stubborn, persistent
obstupefaciō, -ere, -fēcī, -factum, to stun, astound, to be dumbfounded

obstupescō, -ere, -stupuī, —, to be struck dumb, dazed
obtegō, -ere, -texī, -tectum, to cover
obtingō, -ere, -tigī, —, to fall to one's lot
obtruncō (1), to cut to pieces, slaughter
obumbrō (1), to cover with shadow, shade
obvius, -a, -um, *adj.*, lying open or exposed
occāsiō, -ōnis, *f.*, occasion, opportunity
occīdō, -ere, -cīdī, -cīsum, to kill, ruin
occipiō, -ere, -cēpī, -ceptum, to begin
occumbō, -ere, -cubuī, —, to fall, lie down, die
oculus, -ī, *m.*, eye
offendō, -ere, -fendī, -fensum, to meet, offend, strike against
offerō, -ferre, obtulī, oblātum, to offer
officīna, -ae, *f.*, workshop
officium, -iī, *n.*, duty, function
offula, -ae, *f.*, a small piece of food
offundō, -ere, -fūdī, -fūsum, to pour out, spread out, tumble down
oleāginus, -a, -um, *adj.*, of an olive
oleum, -ī, *n.*, oil
olla, -ae, *f.*, pot
ollula, -ae, *f.*, a small pot (diminutive of **olla**)

omittō, -ere, -mīsī, -missum, to leave off, stop

omnīno, *adv.*, altogether, entirely

omnis, -e, *adj.*, all

onustus, -a, -um, *adj.*, burdened

opācus, -a, -um, *adj.*, dark

operculum, -ī, *n.*, cover, lid

opīmus, -a, -um, *adj.*, choice, rich

opīniō, -ōnis, *f.*, opinion, reputation

optimus, -a, -um, best (superl. of **bonus**)

optō (1), to desire

ōrāculum, -ī, *n.*, divine utterance

orbis, orbis, *m.*, circle

orchestra, -ae, *f.*, the area in front of the stage in a theater

Orcus, -ī, *m.*, god of the infernal regions, another name for Dis, Pluto

ordeum, -ī, *n.*, barley

ordō, -inis, *m.*, row, line; **per ordinem**, in order

orīginālis, -e, *adj.*, existing at the beginning, causing beginnings, originative

orīgō, -inis, *f.*, beginning, origin, ancestry

ōrō (1), to pray, beseech, supplicate

ōs, ōris, *n.*, mouth, face

os, ossis, *n.*, bone

osculor, -ārī, -ātus sum, to kiss

osculum, -ī, *n.*, kiss

Osīris, -is, *m.*, Osiris, important Egyptian god, husband of Isis

ostensiō, -ōnis, *f.*, a showing (first in Apuleius)

ostentum, -ī, *n.*, a portent, prodigy

ostium, -iī, *n.*, door

ōtiōsē, *adv.*, at one's leisure, tranquilly

pābulum, -ī, *n.*, animal food, fodder

paeniteō, -ēre, -uī, —, to cause to repent, regret (impers. construction + gen. of cause of regret, acc. of person)

palea, -ae, *f.*, chaff, husk

pallium, -iī, *n.*, cloak

pallor, -ōris, *m.*, paleness

palmula, -ae, *f.*, palm of the hand

palpebra, -ae, *f.*, eyelid

Pamphilē, -ēs (Greek forms), *f.*, Pamphile (Milo's wife)

pānis, -is, *m.*, bread

Pāniscus, -ī, *m.*, Paniscus, a little Pan, a minor rural deity

pannulus, -ī, *m.*, a scrap of cloth

pannus, -ī, *m.*, rag

Paphos, -ī (Greek forms), *f.*, Paphos, a city on Cyprus sacred to Venus

papilla, -ae, *f.*, nipple, breast

papȳrus, -ī, *f.*, papyrus plant, papyrus

pār, *gen.* **paris,** *adj.,* equal

parasītus, -ī, *m.,* a table-companion

pārens, -entis, *m./f.,* parent

pariēs, -etis, *m.,* wall

pariō, -ere, peperī, partum, to give birth, bear

parō (1), to prepare

pars, -tis, *f.,* portion, part

partiārius, -a, -um, *adj.,* sharing, shared

partim, *adv.,* partly

partus, -ūs, *m.,* birth, offspring, a birthing, delivery

parvitās, -ātis, *f.,* smallness

parvulus, -a, -um, *adj.,* very small, tiny

parvus, -a, -um, *adj.,* small

pascuae† (textual crux; perhaps having to do with pasture)

passim, *adv.,* here and there

pastophorus, -ī, *m.,* priest of Isis

pastor, -oris, *m.,* shepherd

patefaciō, -ere, -fēcī, -factum, to open

patior, -ī, passus sum, to allow, experience, bear

patrōcinium, -ī, *n.,* patronage, defense in a court of justice

patrōnus, -ī, *m.,* patron

patulus, -a, -um, *adj.,* wide-open, gaping

pauculus, -a, -um, *adj.,* few (diminutive of **paucus**)

paucus, -a, -um, *adj.,* small, few

paulātim, *adv.,* gradually

paulisper, *adv.,* briefly

paululum, *adv.,* slightly, by a brief distance

pauper, *gen.* **-eris,** *adj.,* poor

pausa, -ae, *f.,* pause, respite

pavor, -ōris, *m.,* fear, dread, thrill, anticipation

pax, pācis, *f.,* peace

pectus, -oris, *n.,* breast, heart

pecū, *n. pl.,* **pecua,** domestic animal

pecuīnus, -a, -um, *adj.,* of sheep or cattle

pecūliātus, -a, -um, *adj.,* well-off

pecūlium, -iī, *n.,* money, property

pelagus, -ī, *n.,* the sea

pendulus, -a, -um, *adj.,* drooping, sagging

penetrō (1), to make one's way into, enter

pēnūria, -ae, *f.,* deficiency

per, *prep.* + *acc.,* through

percieō, -ēre, -ciī, -citum, to stir up, excite

percolō, -ere, -uī, -cultum, to cultivate, honor

percutiō, -ere, -cussī, -cussum, to strike

perditus, -a, -um, *adj.,* ruined, lost

perdō, -ere, -didī, -ditum, to destroy

perdoceō, -ēre, -docuī, -doctum, to teach thoroughly

perdūcō, -ere, -dūxī, -ductum, to conduct, bring, drink off, drain

peregrīnātiō, -ōnis, *f.*, foreign travel

pereō, -īre, -iī *or* **-īvī, -itum,** to be lost, perish

pererrō (1), to wander through

perfacile, *adv.*, very easily

perfectus, -a, -um, *adj.*, mature, completed, perfect

perferō, -ferre, -tulī, -lātum, to carry through

perficiō, -ere, -fēcī, -fectum, to finish, render, make; **perficio ut,** to bring it about that

perfidia, -ae, *f.*, treachery, falsehood

perfidus, -a, -um, *adj.*, false, deceitful

perfodiō, -ere, -fōdī, -fossum, to pierce, stab through

perfricō, -āre, -uī, -ātum *or* **-frictum,** to rub all over

perfruor, -ī, -fructus sum, to enjoy to the fullest

perfundō, -ere, -fūdī, -fūsum, to suffuse

pergō, -ere, perrexī, perrectum, to move toward

perīclitābundus, -a, -um, *adj.*, testing (only in Apuleius)

perīculum, -ī, *n.*, danger

perimō, -ere, perēmī, peremptum, to kill

perlinō, -ere, -lēvī, -litum, to smear all over

permisceō, -ēre, -miscuī, -mixtum, to mix

permittō, -ere, -mīsī, -missum, to let, allow

permulceō, -ēre, -mulsī, -mulsum, to caress, soothe

perniciēs, -ēī, *f.*, destruction

perniciter, *adv.*, quickly, nimbly

perpetior, -ī, -pessus sum, to undergo

perpetuō, *adv.*, permanently

perpetuus, -a, -um, *adj.*, continual, life-long

perquam, *adv.*, exceedingly

persōna, -ae, *f.*, mask, character, individual

personō, -āre, -uī, -ātum, to cause to resound, to sing loudly

perspergō, -ere, -spersī, -spersum, to sprinkle

perstrepō, -ere, to make a place resound with noise

pertrectō (1), to handle

pervādō, -ere, -vāsī, -vāsum, to spread

pervagor, -ārī, -ātus sum, to wander about

perveniō, -īre, -vēnī, -ventum, to come to, reach

pēs, pedis, *m.*, foot

pessimus, -a, -um, *adj.*, worst

petō, -ere, -īvī *or* **-iī, -ītum,** to seek, direct one's course to

petulans, *gen.* **-ntis,** *adj.*, wanton, immodest

phalerae, -ārum, *f. pl.*, metal disk worn as ornament by horses, trappings

pharetra, -ae, *f.*, quiver

philosophus, -ī, *m.*, philosopher

Phoebus, -ī, *m.,* Phoebus
(Apollo)

Phōtis, -idis, *f.,* Fotis

piāmentum, -ī, *n.,* expiatory
rite

piger, -gra, -grum, *adj.,*
sluggish

pignerō (1), to bind

pilus, -ī, *m.,* hair

pinna, -ae, *f.,* feather, wing

pinnātus, -a, -um, *adj.,*
winged

pinnula, -ae, *f.,* a little wing

placeō, -ēre, -uī, -itum, to be
pleasing (+ dat.)

placidē, *adv.,* calmly

plācō (1), to appease,
propitiate

plāgōsus, -a, -um, *adj.,* much-
beaten

plānē, *adv.,* clearly, utterly

plangor, -ōris, *m.,* lamentation

planta, -ae, *f.,* sole of the foot

platea, -ae, *f.,* street

plebs, -ēbis, *f.,* the general
populace

plērusque, -aque, -umque, *adj.,*
the greater part, most of, a
great number, very many

plūmō (1), to be or become
covered with feathers

plūmula, -ae, *f.,* a little feather

plūrimus, -a, -um, *superl. adj.,*
the greatest number of, very
many

plusculus, -a, -um, *adj.,*
somewhat larger, largish

Plūtarchus, -ī, *m.,* Plutarch, a
Greek author

pōcillātor, -ōris, *m.,* cupbearer
(only in Apuleius)

pōculum, -ī, *n.,* a drinking cup

poētica, -ae, *f.,* the poetic art

pollens, *gen.* **-ntis,** *adj.,* strong

polleō, -ēre, —, —, to be
powerful, be strong

pollex, -icis, *m.,* the thumb

pōmērium, -iī, *n.,* the
"pomerium," the boundary
of a town

pondus, -eris, *n.,* weight

pōne, *adv.,* behind

pōnō, -ere, posuī, positum, to
place

poples, -itis, *m.,* the knee, knee-
joint

populus, -ī, *m.,* the people,
community

porrigō, -ere, -rexī, -rectum,
to stretch out, spread out,
offer

**portendō, -ere, -tendī,
-tentum,** to portend

portus, -ūs, *m.,* harbor

possideō, -ēre, -sēdī, -sessum,
to have, possess

possum, posse, potuī, —, to be
able

post, *prep.* + *acc.,* after

postlīminium, -iī, *n.,*
resumption of civic
rights; (abl.) back again;
postliminio mortis, back
from death

**postpōnō, -ere, -posuī,
-positum,** to postpone

postrēmus, -a, -um, *adj.,* lower,
last

postumus, -a, -um, *adj.*, last, final

potentia, -ae, *f.*, power

potior, -īrī, -ītus sum, to be powerful, have control, possess

potior, -or, -us, *compar. adj.*, more powerful

potissimum, *adv.*, especially

praebeō, -ēre, -uī, -itum, to present, supply

praebibō, -ere, -ī, -itum, to drink as a toast, drink to one's health

praecaveō, -ēre, -cāvī, -cautum, to beware

praecēdō, -ere, -cessī, -cessum, to precede, come at an earlier time

praeceps, -cipitis, *n.*, the highest part, summit, precipice

praeceptum, -ī, *n.*, instruction, order

praecipitō (1), to hurl down, leap down

praecipuē, *adv.*, especially

praecipuus, -a, -um, *adj.*, exceptional, special

praeclārus, -a, -um, *adj.*, splendid, radiant, famous

praeda, -ae, *f.*, booty, prey

praedicō (1), to predict, warn

praeditus, -a, -um, *adj.*, possessed of

praeeō, -īre, -īvī *or* **-iī, —,** lead, guide

praeferō, -ferre, -tulī, -lātum, to prefer

praefor, -ārī, -fātus sum, to request in advance (+ acc.)

praemicō, -are, to gleam brightly

praemium, -iī, *n.*, reward

praeniteō, -ēre, -uī, —, to shine brightly

praeparō (1), to prepare

praepotens, *gen.* **-ntis,** *adj.*, very powerful

praesāgium, -iī, *n.*, a forewarning, portent

praesens, *gen.* **-ntis,** *adj.*, present (of time or place), in person, at hand

praesentia, -ae, *f.*, presence

praesēpium, -iī, *n.*, stall for cattle

praevertō, -ere, -vertī, -versum, to forestall

premō, -ere, pressī, pressum, to pursue, afflict

prendō, -ere, prendī, prensum, to grasp

pretium, -iī, *n.* price

prex, precis, *f.*, prayer, entreaty

prīmō, *adv.*, at first

prīmōris, -e, *adj.*, first, leading

prīmum, *adv.*, first; **ut primum,** as soon as

prīmus, -a, -um, *adj.*, first

prior, -or, -us, *compar. adj.*, front, earlier

priscus, -a, -um, *adj.*, ancient

pristinus, -a, -um, *adj.*, old, former

priusquam, *adv.*, before

prīvō (1), (+ abl.), to deprive of

prō, *interj.,* an exclamation of wonder or lamentation, Oh!, Ah! (+ nom. or vocative)

probus, -a, -um, *adj.,* excellent, able, having an upright character

prōcēdō, -ere, -cessī, -cessum, to go forward, proceed, spring forth

procella, -ae, *f.,* wind, storm

prōcērus, -a, -um, *adj.,* tall, long

procul, *adv.,* far away

prōcurrō, -ere, -cucurrī, -cursum, to rush forward

prōdō, -ere, -didī, -ditum, to bring forth, establish, betray

prōdūcō, -ere, -dūxī, -ductum, to lead forward, lead

proelium, -iī, *n.,* battle

profānō (1), to desecrate

profectō, *adv.,* really, truly

prōferō, -ferre, -tulī, -lātum, to bring out, hold out, extend

profundum, -ī, *n.,* the deep sea

prōgeniēs, -ēī, *f.,* offspring

prōgressus, -ūs, *m.,* the act of going out of the house, an outing

proin, *adv.,* accordingly

prōlixus, -a, -um, *adj.,* extended, long

prōmicō (1), to shoot forth, sprout

prōmissum, -ī, *n.,* promise

prōmoveō, -ēre, -mōvī, -mōtum, to make progress

prōnuntiō (1), to proclaim, pronounce

prōnus, -a, -um, *adj.,* leaning or bending forward, moving toward setting

propāgō (1), to produce, reproduce

properē, *adv.,* quickly

propitiō (1), to win over, make favorable, propitiate

propitius, -a, -um, *adj.,* propitious, well-disposed

proprius, -a, -um, *adj.,* one's own, proper

propter, *prep.* + *acc.,* near

prorsum, *adv., See* **prorsus**

prorsus, *adv.,* altogether, quite, absolutely (intensifying a word or phrase)

prōsāpia, -ae, *f.,* lineage, family

proscaenium, -iī, *n.,* the stage

prōsequor, -ī, -secūtus sum, to accompany, follow, honor with (+ abl)

Prōserpina, -ae, *f.,* Proserpina, Persephone, queen of the underworld

prosperus, -a, -um, *adj.,* successful, prosperous

prospicuus, -a, -um, *adj.,* able to look into the future, prophetic

prōsum, prodesse, profuī, to help, to be advantageous

prōterō, -ere, -trīvī, -trītum, to tread underfoot

prōtinus, *adv.,* immediately

prōvidentia, -ae, *f.,* providence, divine guiding force

prōvincia, -ae, *f.,* province, assigned task

prōvolō (1), to fly forth

proximō, -āre, to approach, come near (+ dat.)

proximus, -a, -um, *adj.*, nearest, next; **in proximo,** close at hand

proxumus. *See* **proximus**

prūdens, *gen.* **-ntis,** *adj.*, exercizing foresight, characterized by good sense, sagacious, clever

prūdentia, -ae, *f.*, practical understanding, wisdom

Psȳchē, -ēs (Greek forms), *f.*, Psyche

pūbēs, -is, *f.*, the private parts

pūblicē, *adv.*, as a community, publicly

pūblicus, -a, -um, *adj.*, public

puella, -ae, *f.*, girl

puer, -erī, *m.*, boy, slave

puerīlis, -e, *adj.*, typical of a boy, boyish

pueritia, -ae, *f.*, boyhood

pugil, -ilis, *m.*, boxer

pugnō (1), to engage in battle, fight

pulchrē, *adv.*, beautifully

pulchritūdō, -inis, *f.*, beauty

pullulō, -āre, -āvī, —, to sprout, spring forth

pulmentum, -ī, *n.*, starter dish of meat or fish

pulpa, -ae, *f.*, choice part of meat

pulsus, -ūs, *m.*, impact, beat or throb of the heart

pulvereus, -a, -um, *adj.*, dusty

pulvīnar, -āris, *n.*, a couch (usually for gods)

pulvisculus, -ī, *m.*, dust, powder

punctulum, -ī, *n.*, a prick or stab

punctus, -ūs, *m.*, a pricking, puncture, puncturing

pungō, -ere, pupugī, punctus, to prick, puncture

pūnicans, -ntis, *adj.*, red

pūpula, -ae, *f.*, pupil of the eye

pūrificō (1), to cleanse, make ceremonially pure

purpureus, -a, -um, *adj.*, radiant, glowing

purpurō, -āre, —, —, to make glow with color, to color

putrēdō, -inis, *f.*, rottenness

Pȳthagorās, -ae, *m.*, Pythagoras, famous philosopher

pyxis, -idis, *f.*, small box

quā, *adv.*, where

quadripēs, -edis, *adj.*, four-footed; *as substantive*, a quadruped, domestic animal

quadruplus, -a, -um, *adj.*, four times as great

quaerō, -ere, quaesiī *or* **quaesīvī, quaesītum,** to ask, seek

quālis, -e, *pron.*, *adj.*, of such a sort; what sort (interrog. or exclamatory)

quam, *adv.*, how!, than

quamquam, *rel. adv.*, although

quamvīs, *adv.*, although

quanquam. *See* **quamquam**

quantum, *adv.*, how much, how great

quāquā, *adv.,* in every place

quasi, *adv.,* as if, as it were

quassō (1), to shake

quatiō, -ere, —, quassum, to shake, brandish, rock, knock

queō, -īre, quīvī, —, to be able

queror, -ī, questus sum, to grumble, complain, protest

querulus, -a, -um, *adj.,* having a plaintive or mournful sound

quī, quae, quod, *rel. pron.,* who, which

quīcumque, quaecumque, quodcumque, *rel. and indef. pron. and adj.,* whoever, whatever

quīdam, quaedam, quiddam, *pron.,* a certain (undefined) person or thing

quīdam, quaedam, quoddam, *adj.,* a certain

quidem, *adv.,* in fact; **ne . . . quidem,** not even

quiēs, -ētis, *f.,* sleep, rest

quiescō, -ere, quiēvī, quiētum, to be at rest

quiētus, -a, -um, *adj.,* calm, restful

quinquennālis, -is, *m.,* an official holding an office in a *collegium*

Quirītēs, -ium, *m. pl.,* Roman citizens

quis, quid, *pron. interrog.,* who, which; *indef.* (after *si, nisi, num, ne*), anyone, anything

quispiam, quaepiam, quodpiam, *adj.,* any, some

quisquam, quicquam, *pron., adj.,* anyone, anything, any

quisquis, quidquid, *adj.,* whoever, whatever

quīvīs, quaevīs, quidvīs, *pron.,* anyone, anything

quoad, *rel. adv.,* until

quod, *conj.,* because

quondam, *adv.,* formerly

quoque, *adv.,* also, besides

quōquōversus, *adv.,* in every direction

rabiēs, -ēī, *f.,* savagery

rādō, -ere, rāsī, rāsum, to shave

rāmus, -ī, *m.,* branch

rārus, -a, -um, *adj.,* rare, exquisite

ratiō, -ōnis, *f.,* reckoning, reason, account, mode, manner, fashion

reābse, *adv.,* really, from the circumstances

recipiō, -ere, -cēpī, -ceptum, to admit, make welcome, admit into friendship

reciprocus, -a, -um, *adj.,* moving backward and forward, alternating, reciprocal

reclūdō, -ere, -clūsī, -clūsum, to open

recondō, -ere, -condidī, -conditum, to put back

recordātiō, -ōnis, *f.,* a recollection

recordor, -ārī, -ātus sum, to call to mind, recollect

recreō (1), to restore, relieve, refresh, to make anew

recurrō, -ere, -currī, -cursum, to run back

reddō, -ere, reddidī, redditum, to give back, render; **iudicium reddere,** administer justice

redeō, -īre, -iī, -itum, to come or go back

refectiō, -ōnis, *f.,* refreshment

referō, -ferre, retulī, relātum, to bring back, move back, return, reply

reficiō, -ere, -fēcī, -fectum, to restore, refresh

reformātiō, -ōnis, *f.,* transformation, metamorphosis

reformō (1), to transform, change

rēgīna, -ae, *f.,* queen

regiō, -ōnis, *f.,* region, area

regnātor, -ōris, *m.,* king, lord

regō, -ere, rexī, rectum, to rule

religiō, -ōnis, *f.,* religious rites

religiōsus, -a, -um, *adj.,* reverent, sacred, pious; *as substantive,* religious devotee

relinquō, -ere, -līquī, -lictum, to leave behind

reluctor, -ārī, -ātus sum, to struggle, resist

remedium, -iī, *n.,* remedy

removeō, -ēre, -mōvī, -mōtum, to remove

renītor, -ī, -nīsus sum, to resist

rennuō, -ere, rennuī, —, to throw back the head as a sign of refusal

renūdō (1), to lay bare, strip of clothing

reor, rērī, ratus sum, to think, believe

repentīnus, -a, -um, *adj.,* sudden

reperiō, -īre, repperī, repertum, to find

repertus, -ūs, *m.,* discovery, finding

repetō, -ere, -īvī, -ītum, to find again, recover

repleō, -ēre, -ēvī, -ētum, to refill

replicō (1), to go back over

reportō (1), to bring back

reputō (1), to consider

rēs, reī, *f.,* thing, fact, matter, property; *pl.,* the physical world

reserō (1), to open

reservō (1), to reserve, keep for (+ dat.)

resideō, -ēre, resēdī, —, to remain seated, sit, return to its original position

residuus, -a, -um, *adj.,* residual, remaining

respectō, -āre, —, —, to look back, keep looking at

respiciō, -ere, -spexī, -spectum, to turn one's gaze on, look back

respondeō, -ēre, -spondī, -sponsum, to answer

restituō, -ere, -stituī, -stitūtum, to give back

restō, -āre, -stitī, —, to remain where one is, stand still

resultō, -āre, to jump, spring back

retegō, -ere, -texī, -tectum, to uncover, reveal

retineō, -ēre, -uī, -tentum, to retain, keep

retrahō, -ere, -traxī, -tractum, to drag back

retrōpendulus, -a, -um, *adj.,* hanging down behind (*hapax*)

retrorsus, -a, -um, *adj.,* facing back

revalescō, -ere, -valuī, —, to recover, revive

revellō, -ere, -vellī, -vulsum, to tear away, remove

revēlō (1), to uncover, unveil, reveal

reverticulum, -ī, *n.,* the coming round again of heavenly bodies or events, return

revertor, -ī, -versus sum, to turn around, to return

revocō (1), to call back

rex, rēgis, *m.,* king

rīma, -ae, *f.,* a crack

rīmor, -ārī, -ātus sum, to examine, scrutinize

rīsus, -ūs, *m.,* laughter

Rīsus, -ūs, *m.,* the god of laughter

rīte, *adv.,* duly, properly

rītus, -ūs, *m.,* rite; **ritu,** in the manner of

rīvulus, -ī, *m.,* a stream

rōborō (1), to strengthen

rōrō (1), to drip with moisture

rōs, -ris, *m.,* dew

rosa, -ae, *f.,* rose

roscidus, -a, -um, *adj.,* wet, dewy

roseus, -a, -um, *adj.,* made of roses, rose-colored

rotō (1), to rotate

rudis, -e, *adj.,* rough, crude, unrefined, unsophisticated

rūmor, -ōris, *m.,* rumor, gossip

rursus, rursum, *adv.,* back again, again

russeus, -a, -um, *adj.,* red

rusticus, -a, -um, *adj.,* rustic, belonging to the country

rutundō *or* **rotundō** (1), to make round

sacerdōs, -ōtis, *m.,* priest

sacrāmentum, -ī, *n.,* oath, allegiance, military oath of allegiance, obligation

sacrārium, -iī, *n.,* sanctuary, shrine

sacrilegus, -a, -um, *adj.,* sacrilegious, impious

sacrum, -ī, *n.,* religious observance, rite, especially secret rites or mysteries

saeculum, -ī, *n.,* a generation, age, century

saepe, *adv.,* often

saeviō, -īre, -iī, -ītum, to rage

saevitia, -ae, *f.,* savagery, cruelty

saevus, -a, -um, *adj.,* savage, cruel

sagitta, -ae, *f.,* arrow

saltem, *adv.*, at least, anyhow

saltō (1), to dance

saltus, -ūs, *m.*, a jump, leap

salūber, -bre, *adj.*, health-giving, salubrious

salūs, -ūtis, *f.*, safety, health, deliverance, security, resource

salūtāris, -e, *adj.*, health-promoting, curative

salvē, hello, farewell

sānē, *adv.*, certainly

sanguis, -inis, *m.*, blood

sapidus, -a, -um, *adj.*, tasty

sarcina, -ae, *f.*, a bundle

satiō (1), to satisfy

satis, *indecl. adv.*, enough, very

Saturus, -ī, *m.*, Saturus, a demi-god of wild places

saucius, -a, -um, *adj.*, wounded

sāvium, -iī, *n.*, a kiss

saxeus, -a, -um, *adj.*, stone-like

scabiōsus, -a, -um, *adj.*, mangy, scabbed

scaena, -ae, *f.*, scene, stage

scaevus, -a, -um, *adj.*, unlucky, ill-omened

scientia, -ae, *f.*, knowledge, understanding, expertise, skill, art

scīlicet, *particle*, evidently, doubtless

sciō, -īre, -iī *or* **-īvī, -ītum,** to know

scissilis, -e, *adj.*, torn

scītē, *adv.*, ingeniously

scītulus, -a, -um, *adj.*, pretty

scrībō, -ere, scrībsī, scriptum, to write, inscribe

sē, sēsē, *pron.*, himself, herself, itself, themselves, him, her, it, them

secō, -āre, -uī, -tum, to cut

sēcrētō, *adv.*, in private

sēcrētum, -ī, *n.*, a secret, mystic rite

sēcrētus, -a, -um, *adj.*, remote, hidden, secret

sēcūrus, -a, -um, *adj.*, untroubled

secus, *adv.*, otherwise

sed, *conj.*, but

sēdēs, -is, *f.*, seat, dwelling

sedīle, -is, *n.*, seat, chair

sēdō (1), to relieve, mitigate

sēmen, -inis, *n.*, seed

sēmiconspicuus, -a, -um, *adj.*, half-visible (hapax)

sēmirāsus, -a, -um, *adj.*, partly shaven

sēmita, -ae, *f.*, path

semper, *adv.*, always

senex, -is, *adj.*, old

sensim, *adv.*, slowly

sensus, -ūs, *m.*, consciousness

sententia, -ae, *f.*, thought, sentence (in court)

septies, *adv.*, seven times

sequor, -ī, secūtus sum, to follow

serēnus, -a, -um, *adj.*, untroubled, reassuring

sermō, -ōnis, *m.*, talk, conversation, way or style of speaking

serō, -ere, seruī, sertum, to bind together, interweave

serpō, -ere, serpsī, to wind, snake along

servīlis, -e, *adj.,* worthy of a slave, servile

serviō, -īre, -īvī *or* **-iī, -itum,** + *dat.,* to serve as a slave, be subject to, tend to

servitium, -iī, *n.,* servitude

servus, -ī, *m.,* slave

sēta, -ae, *f.,* the hair of an animal

seu. *See* **sive**

Sextus, -ī, *m.,* Sextus the philospher, Plutarch's nephew

sexus, -ūs, *m.,* sex, gender

sī, *conj.,* if

sīc, *adv.,* thus, so, in this way

silentiōsus, -a, -um, *adj.,* noiseless, tranquil

silentium, -iī, *n.,* silence

similis, -e, *adj.,* similar, like

similiter, *adv.,* in a similar manner

similitūdō, -inis, *f.,* similarity, resemblance

simul, *adv.,* at the same time, simultaneously, together with

simulācrum, -ī, *n.,* likeness, statue

sine, *prep.* + *abl.,* without

singulāris, -e, *adj.,* remarkable

singulī, -ae, -a, *pl. adj.,* each one, single, one by one

singultiō, -īre, —, —, to sob

sinister, -tra, -trum, *adj.,* left, unlucky, adverse

sinus, -ūs, *m.,* breast, embrace

sīquis, sīquid, *indef. pron.,* if anyone, if any (**sī** + **quis**)

sistō, -ere, stetī *or* **stitī, statum,** to set up, place

sitiō, -īre, —, —, to be thirsty

situs, -ūs, *m.,* position, situation

sīve, seu, or if; **sīve . . . sīve,** whether . . . or

sociō (1), to unite (in marriage, vel sim.)

sodālis, -is, *m.,* a companion

sōl, sōlis, *m.* the sun

sōlācium, -iī, *n.,* consolation

solidus, -a, -um, *adj.,* unbroken, healed

sōlitūdō, -inis, *f.,* loneliness, emptiness

sollemniter, *adv.,* with due ritual

sōlor, -ārī, -ātus sum, to solace, comfort

sōlus, -a, -um, *adj.,* alone, solitary

solūtus, -a, -um, *adj.,* loose

somnior, -ārī, —, to dream

somnus, -ī, *m.,* sleep

sōpiō, -īre, -īvī, -ītum, to lull to sleep

sopor, -ōris, *m.,* sleep

sordēs, -is, *f.,* dirt, filth

sordidē, *adv.,* squalidly

soror, -ōris, *f.,* sister

sors, -rtis, *f.,* fortune, destiny, lot

spargō, -ere, sparsī, sparsum, to scatter

sparteus, -a, -um, *adj.,* made of rope

Spartiāticus, -a, -um, *adj.,* Spartan

spatium, -iī, *n.,* length

speciēs, -ēī, *f.*, aspect, form, appearance

specimen, -inis, *n.*, sight, manifestation

spectāculum, -ī, *n.*, sight

specula, -ae, *f.*, the act of observing or spying on

spernō, -ere, sprēvī, sprētum, to reject, spurn

spēs, speī, *f.*, hope

spīna, -ae, *f.*, spine, backbone

spīrō (1), to breathe

spissus, -a, -um, *adj.*, thick and fast

splendidus, -a, -um, *adj.*, splendid, illustrious

splendor, -ōris, *m.*, brightness, brilliance

sponte, *abl. of* **spons,** of one's own free will

spūmō (1), to foam, froth

squāleō, -ēre, -uī, —, to be rough or filthy

stabulō (1), to be housed in a stable

stabulum, -ī, *n.*, a stable

statim, *adv.*, immediately

statua, -ae, *f.*, a statue

statuō, -ere, statuī, statutum, to decide

stilla, -ae, *f.*, a drop

stilus, -ī, *m.*, stylus (pen), mode of composition, style

stimulus, -ī, *m.*, a goad, prick

stīpendium, -iī, *n.*, military campaign

stīpō (1), to pack

stips, stipis, *f.*, a small offering of money

stō, stāre, stetī, statum, to stand

strīdor, -ōris, *m.*, a screech

studiōsus, -a, -um, *adj.*, eager, zealous

studium, -iī, *n.*, eagerness, desire, intellectual study

stupidus, -a, -um, *adj.*, dazed, shocked

stupor, -ōris, *m.*, bewilderment, stupefaction

Stygius, -a, -um, *adj.*, Stygian, of the Underworld

suādeō, -ēre, suāsī, suāsum, to persuade, urge

suāvis, -e, *adj.*, pleasant, sweet

sub, *prep. + abl. or acc.*, under, below, during

subdolus, -a, -um, *adj.*, treacherous

subitō, *adv.*, suddenly

subitus, -a, -um, *adj.*, sudden

sublīmō (1), to raise; *pass.*, to soar

subministrō (1), to assist

subolēs, -is, *f.*, offspring, progeny

subsistō, -ere, substitī, (+ dat.), to remain, tarry, support

subtīlis, -e, *adj.*, well-timed, well-judged

succinctulus, -a, -um, *adj.*, girded, belted

succumbō, -ere, -cubuī, -cubitum, to submit

succurrō, -ere, -currī, -cursum, to bring help, aid

successus, -ūs, *m.*, a shaking, jolting

succutiō, -ere, -cussī, -cussum, to shake

sufferō, -ferre, sustūlī, sublātum, to offer, give, endure, raise up

sufficienter, *adv.*, sufficiently

suffigō, -ere, -fixī, -fixum, to fix underneath as a support

sum, esse, fuī, futurus, to be

summa, -ae, *f.*, purpose, tendency

summās, *gen.* **-ātis,** *adj.*, belonging to the highest rank

summergō, -ere, -mersī, -mersum, to submerge

summittō, -ere, -mīsī, -missum, to drop, lower

summus, -a, -um, *adj.*, highest

sūmō, -ere, sumpsī, sumptum, to take

super, *adv.* + *acc.*, over, above

superingredior, -ī, -gressus sum, to enter on a cue (hapax)

superior, -us, *compar. adj.*, higher

supernatō, -āre, to float

suppeditō (1), to be available

suppetiae, -ārum, *f. pl.*, aid, relief

supplicō (1), to make offerings, worship

suscipiō, -ere, -cēpī, -ceptum, to take up, receive

suscitō (1), to rouse from sleep, revive

suspendō, -ere, -pendī, -pensum, to raise up, be in suspense

suspiciō, -ere, -spexī, -spectum, to look at, honor

sustineō, -ēre, -uī, —, to endure

susurrus, -ī, *m.*, whisper

suus, -a, -um, *adj.*, his, her, their own

Sulla, -ae, *m.*, Sulla

tacitus, -a, -um, *adj.*, silent

Taenaros, -ī (Greek forms), *f.*, Taenarus, a promontory in Laconia

tālis, -e, *adj.*, such, of such a kind

tam, *adv.*, so

tamen, *adv.*, nevertheless, however, all the same

tandem, *adv.*, finally, at length

tantillus, -a, -um, *adj.*, so small a quantity

tantum, *adv.*, so much, only; **tantum modo,** only

tantus, -a, -um, *adj.*, so great, so much as

tardus, -a, -um, *adj.*, slow, late

tectum, -ī, *n.*, building

tegīle, -is, *n.*, covering (hapax)

tegmen, -inis, *n.*, covering, skin

tēlum, -ī, *n.*, weapon

temerārius, -a, -um, *adj.*, reckless, impetuous

temperō (1), to refrain, hold back from

tempestās, -ātis, *f.*, storm

templum, -ī, *n.*, temple

temporālis, -e, *adj.*, temporary

temptō (1), to try, try to attain

tempus, -oris, *n.*, time

tēmulentus, -a, -um, *adj.,*
  drunken, soaked
tenebrae, -ārum, *f. pl.,*
  darkness
tenellus, -a, -um, *adj.,* tender,
  delicate
teneō, -ēre, -uī, -tum, to hold,
  occupy
tenuō (1), to make thin
tenus, *prep. + preceding gen.,* as
  far as, right down to
terminō (1), to conclude
terminus, -ī, *m.,* end
terra, -ae, *f.,* land, ground,
  earth
terrēnus, -a, -um, *adj.,* earthly
testor, -ārī, -ātus sum, to bear
  witness to
textrix, -īcis, *f.,* female weaver
theātrum, -ī, *n.,* theater
Thessalia, -ae, *f.,* Thessaly, a
  region of Greece
tībia, -ae, *f.,* a musical pipe,
  woodwind instrument
timor, -ōris, *m.,* fear
titubō (1), to stagger
tolerō (1), to bear, hold, tolerate
tollō, -ere, sustulī, sublātum,
  to pick up, raise
torus, -ī, *m.,* bed
tot, *adv.,* so many
tōtus, -a, -um, *adj.,* the whole
  of, all
tractō (1), to drag, treat, deal
  with
trādō, -ere, -didī, -ditum, to
  hand over, give oneself to
trahō, -ere, traxī, tractum, to
  drag

transeō, -īre, -īvī, -itum, to go
  across
transferō, -ferre, -tulī, -latum,
  to change, transform
transigō, -ere, transēgī,
  transactum, to spend
translātiō, -ōnis, *f.,* transfer
transmittō, -ere, -mīsī,
  -missum, to cross, traverse
tremō, -ere, -uī, —, to tremble,
  shake
tremulē, *adv.,* quiveringly,
  restlessly
tremulus, -a, -um, *adj.,* shaking
trepidātiō, -ōnis, *f.,* state of
  alarm, trepidation
trepidō (1), to quiver with
  excitement
trepidus, -a, -um, *adj.,*
  apprehensive, shaking
trēs, trēs, tria, *pl. adj.,* three
tribuō, -ere, tribuī, tribūtum,
  to grant, bestow
triformis, -e, *adj.,* having three
  forms
trīnī, -ae, -a, *pl. adj.,* triple
tristitūdō, -inis, *f.,* sadness,
  gloom (only in Apuleius)
trītūra, -ae, *f.,* rubbing, friction
trūdō, -ere, trūsī, trūsum, to
  push, shove
tū, *pron.,* you
tuccētum, -ī, *n.,* some savory
  dish
tum, *adv.,* then
tunc, *adv.,* then
tunica, -ae, *f.,* tunic
tunicātus, -a, -um, *adj.,*
  wearing a tunic

turba, -ae, *f.,* crowd
turris, -is, *f.,* tower
tussēdō, -inis, *f.,* a cough
tūtēla, -ae, *f.,* protection
tuus, -a, -um, *adj.,* your

ūbertim, *adv.,* copiously
ubī, *adv.,* where, when
ubīque, *adv.,* anywhere, everywhere
ūdus, -a, -um, *adj.,* wet
ullus, -a, -um, *adj.,* any at all, any
ultimus, -a, -um, *adj.,* last
ultrō, *adv.,* voluntarily, of one's own accord
ululātus, -ūs, *m.,* howling
umerus, -ī, *m.,* shoulder
ūmidus, -a, -um, *adj.,* damp
umquam, *adv.,* ever
unctulum, -ī, *n.,* small amount of ointment (hapax)
unctum, -ī, *n.,* ointment
undique, *adv.,* from all sides; **undique versum** (sometimes as one word), from every direction or angle
undō (1), to move like a wave, undulate
unguēdō, -inis, *f.,* an ointment or unguent (hapax)
unguis, -is, *m.,* fingernail, claw
ungula, -ae, *f.,* hoof
ūnicus, -a, -um, *adj.,* one and only
ūniformis, -e, *adj.,* contained in a single form
ūnus, -a, -um, *adj.,* one
urbs, urbis, *f.,* city, town

ūrō, -ere, ussī, ustum, to burn
uspiam, *adv.,* somewhere, anywhere
usquam, *adv.,* anywhere
ūsurpō (1), to take possession of, assume
ut, *adv., conj.,* as, when, how, in order that, with the result that
utcumque, *adv.,* in any event, at any rate
uter, utris, *m.,* leather bag, wine-skin
uterque, utraque, utrumque, *adj., pron.,* each of two
utinam, *particle,* if only, how I wish that
uxor, -ōris, *f.,* wife

vacillō (1), to be unsteady, flicker
vādō, -ere, vāsī, —, to go; **pedibus vadere in sententiam,** to make one's support known by walking to a side
valdē, *adv.,* extremely, assuredly
vallēs, -is, *f.,* valley
vapōrōsus, -a, -um, *adj.,* full of steam or vapor
varius, -a, -um, *adj.,* numerous and varied, changing
vasculum, -ī, *n.,* small vessel or container
vāticinātiō, -onis, *f.,* prophecy
vēcors, *gen.* **-rdis,** *adj.,* frenzied
vector, -ōris, *m.,* a carrier, bearer

vegetō, -āre, to invigorate

vegetus, -a, -um, *adj.,* vigorous, energetic

vehementer, *adv.,* strongly

vel, *conj., adv.,* or, even, perhaps

vēlitor, -ārī, -ātus sum, to skirmish

vēlox, *gen.* **-ōcis,** *adj.,* swift

velut, *adv.,* like, as if

venerātiō, -ōnis, *f.,* worship

venerius, -a, -um, *adj.,* of the goddess Venus, sexual

veneror, -ārī, -ātus sum, to worship, revere, hold in awe

venia, -ae, *f.,* a favor, indulgence

veniō, -īre, vēnī, ventum, to come, appear

venter, -tris, *m.,* belly

Venus, -eris, *f.,* Venus, goddess of love and beauty

venustās, -ātis, *f.,* charm, grace

verber, -eris, *n.,* a whip, a flogging, blow

verbum, -ī, *n.,* word

vērē, *adv.,* truly

vereor, -ērī, -itus sum, to fear, show reverence

vērō, *adv.,* really, without doubt

versum. *See* **undique**

vērum, *adv.,* truly, but, but also

vērus, -a, -um, *adj.,* real, true

vesper, -erī, *m.,* evening; **vesperī,** in the evening

vespernus, -a, -um, *adj.,* of the evening

vespertīnus, -a, -um, *adj.,* of the evening

vester, -tra, -trum, *adj.,* your (pl.)

vestīgium, -iī, *n.,* footstep, step, trace

vestis, -is, *f.,* dress, clothing

veternus, -ī, *m.,* dirt

vetus, *gen.* **-eris,** *adj.,* old, long-established

vetustus, -a, -um, *adj.,* ancient

via, -ae, *f.,* road, journey

vībex, -īcis, *f.,* a sore

vibrō (1), to move to and fro

vicārius, -a, -um, *adj.,* substitute

vicis (*gen.*), turn, exchange; **in . . . vicem** *or* **vice** (+ gen.), in place of

vicissitūdō, -inis, *f.,* alternation

victima, -ae, *f.,* victim (in animal sacrifice)

videō, -ēre, vīdī, vīsum, to see

viduitās, -ātis, *f.,* widowhood

viduus, -a, -um, *adj.,* deprived of a spouse, widowed, bereft

vigilia, -ae, *f.,* a "watch," one of the divisions of the night

vigilō (1), to stay awake, be awake

vīlis, -e, *adj.,* cheap, humble

vindicō (1), to assert one's claim to, claim as free, liberate, rescue

vindicta, -ae, *f.,* vengeance

vīnum, -ī, *n.,* wine

violentia, -ae, *f.,* force

vir, virī, *m.,* man

vireō, -ēre, -uī, —, to be vigorous

virginālis, -e, *adj.,* maidenly

virgō, -inis, *f.*, girl of marriageable age, maiden

virtūs, -ūtis, *f.* valor, excellence, goodness, ability

vīs, *pl.* **vīrium,** *f.*, force, strength

viscum *or* **viscus, -eris,** *n.*, meat, internal organs

vīsō, -ere, vīsī, to look

vīta, -ae, *f.*, life

vītō (1), to avoid

vīvō, -ere, vīxī, victum, to live

vix, *adv.*, scarcely

vocō (1), to call

volātilis, -e, *adj.*, equipped for flying, able to fly

volātus, -ūs, *m.*, flight

volens, *gen.* **-ntis,** *adj.*, willing

volō, velle, voluī, —, to want

volō (1), to fly

voluptāriē, *adv.*, pleasurably

voluptās, -ātis, *f.*, pleasure, joy

Voluptās, -ātis, *f.*, Joy

volūtātus, -ūs, *m.*, a rolling, wallowing

vōs, *pron.*, you (pl.)

vōtum, -ī, *n.*, desire, hope

vox, vōcis, *f.*, voice, language

Vulcānus, -ī, *m.*, Vulcan, god of fire

vulnerō (1), to wound

vulnus, -eris, *n.*, wound

vulturius, -iī, *m.*, vulture

vultus, -ūs, *m.*, face

ℬℭ LATIN Readers

Series Editor: RONNIE ANCONA, HUNTER COLLEGE
AND CUNY GRADUATE CENTER